ROUTER BENCH GUIDE

Zachary Taylor

STERLING PUBLISHING CO. INC., NEW YORK

10 9 8 7 6 5 4 3 2 1

Series Editor: Michael Cea
Series Designer: Chris Swirnoff

Published 2002 by Sterling Publishing Company, Inc.
387 Park Avenue South, New York, New York 10016
Originally published under the title *Router: Workshop Bench reference*
© 1999 by Zachary Taylor
Distributed in Canada by Sterling Publishing
c/o Canadian Manda Group, One Atlantic Avenue, Suite 105
Toronto, Ontario, Canada M6K 3E7
Distributed in Great Britain and Europe by Cassell PLC
Wellington House, 125 Strand, London WC2R 0BB, England
Distributed in Australia by Capricorn Link (Australia) Pty. Ltd.
P.O. Box 704, Windsor, NSW 2756 Australia
Printed in China
All rights reserved

Sterling ISBN 0-8069-8933-5

Dedication

To Jim Phillips

*I dedicate this book to you Jim, as a token of respect for the part
you have played in the development of the versatility of the router.
You recognized its potential before most of us had even seen one.
Your contributions to routing are immeasurable as pioneer, designer, developer, instructor, and author. Many router users benefiting
from your work may not even know your name. To those who do,
you are already a legend.*

Zachary Taylor

Acknowledgments

Thanks are due to the following people and companies, who in one way or another helped in the preparation of this book:

Jean-Pierre Bellanger, of Bridonneau, France, for router cutters;

Black & Decker, for routers and accessories;

Manny Cefai, for some photography;

Cristina Di Staola, of CMT Utensili SRL, Italy, for router cutters and accessories;

DeWalt, for routers and accessories;

Roger Buse, of Hegner, UK, for Unicut radial arm routing attachment;

Arthur Taverner, of Hitachi Power Tools, UK, for routers and attachments;

Ian Small, of KWO Tools Ltd., UK, for router cutters;

Ramon Weston, of Leigh Industries Ltd., UK, for dovetail jigs;

Tobias Cardew, of lo-tec pieman Ltd., UK, for V-Mach vacuum clamps;

Pat Lovell, of P. Lovell Workwear, UK, for overalls and protective clothing;

Terry Bicker, of Makita Ltd., UK, for routers and accessories;

Paul Merry, of M&M Distributors, UK, for Titan Cutters, and accessories;

Jack Garlick, of Porter Cable Hamilton Power, for routers and accessories;

Stephen Phillips, of Trend Machinery and Cutting Tools, UK, for routers, cutters, and accessories and for the use of photographs and illustrations;

Alan Arnott, of Wealdon Tool Co., Uk, for router cutters and accessories;

Martin Godfrey, of Woodrat, UK, for jigs, router cutters, and accessories.

Contents

Introduction

It is difficult to describe fully the sense of satisfaction that comes from the joining of one piece of wood to another. Whether the objective is to make a simple box or create a magnificent cabinet, there is an elated feeling of fulfillment when the aim is achieved. Correct procedures coupled with properly chosen materials are essential, and somewhere within the formula there comes the selection of the appropriate tools for the job. In the vast array of woodworking tools, there is one that offers more solutions to the problems of cutting and shaping wood than any other. It is the router.

Among the adjectives that have been used to describe the router—"incredible," "amazing," "remarkable," "practical," etc.— the word most likely to appeal to its user, or to a prospective owner, is "versatile." No other power tool is capable of as many woodworking functions.

More than half a century ago, electric drills were well established in the domestic sector as a means of boring holes in walls, ceilings, and floors. Routers are following in those footsteps — not surprisingly, since they are a similar type of machine but with so many applications as to be beyond listing. Drilling holes is but one of hundreds of a router's applications.

Just as the electric drill needs drill bits to function, so the router needs cutters. Most of the latter are designed to create joints meeting the needs of the carpenter, joiner, and cabinetmaker, plus some "special" ones devised to achieve quick results in kitchens and other domestic situations. Some routers perform as mini spindle molders able to shape moldings, while others have been

Author Zachary Taylor

developed for decorative effects. Chapter 2 describes a wide range of cutters.

When combined with accessories selected from the huge range currently available, the role of the router may be extended into the world of production and high precision. Such accessories are described in the following pages.

With a price tag as low as a decent meal for four, an entry-level router will quickly earn its keep in practical hands that have many woodworking projects to perform. Purely as a workshop space-saver, the router tops the list, since it can duplicate the performance of many bigger, more expensive machines, yet it occupies little more room than a coffeepot.

All power tools are potentially dangerous, but with correct procedures and the observation of simple but essential safety rules, risks with the router may be minimized. These rules are described in Chapter 10.

Wide-ranging applications require the prospective owner to assess the uses to which the router will be put, in order that the correct choice be made of machine, cutters, and associated equipment.

Most people using the router are inspired to concoct some special application or home-spun attachment to suit a particular need, and by such means new techniques are emerging all the time to further extend the machine's range of operations. Chapter 9 describes various jigs and fixtures that will help extend your router's capabilities.

The router is probably the chief tool to inspire those who lack confidence with conventional hand tools, those who protest their inabilities by declaring their fingers to be "all thumbs." They should be mindful of the fellow who was an expert with the router, despite the fact that he hadn't any thumbs at all!

This book is intended to show the range of applications available to the router owner, and a glance will tell the reader just how vast that range can be. Enthusiasts are encouraged to contact the many suppliers of machinery, cutters, and accessories to better know what is available currently and to help determine the most suitable equipment for their needs. The world of the router is inspiringly progressive.

Router Components and Features

Operating Principles

A router (1–1) is an electrically powered machine comprising a motor, attached to the spindle of which is a collet, or chuck, into which may be inserted rotary cutting bits (normally referred to as cutters). Being, in principle, a portable tool, the router's orientation depends on its application, but when operated by hand, the router normally is used with the motor spindle vertical and with the cutter pointing down. It may be suspended in this position by a bracket permitting

1–1. An assortment of plunge routers, taken from the scores currently available. Plunge routers are discussed on pages 19 and 20.

so-called "overhead" routing (1–2 to 1–4) or it may be inverted and attached to a table with the cutter protruding through a suitable hole for "inverted" routing. In both of these applications (which are described in Chapter 5), the hands are freed from contact with the router, being used to

"OVERHEAD" ROUTING

1–2. Designed to hold power tools—in this case the router in overhead mode—this radial-arm tool will also accept a power saw or angle grinder.

1–3. Dedicated to accommodate the router in many positions, this equipment is being used to hold the router in overhead mode. In this view, the router is at its lowest position and close to the upright pillar on which it is supported.

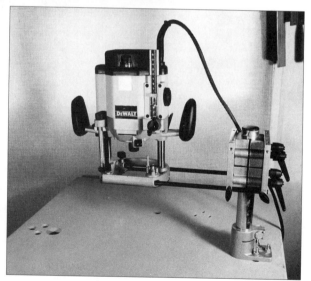

1–4. Here the router is at its highest position and farthest from the pillar.

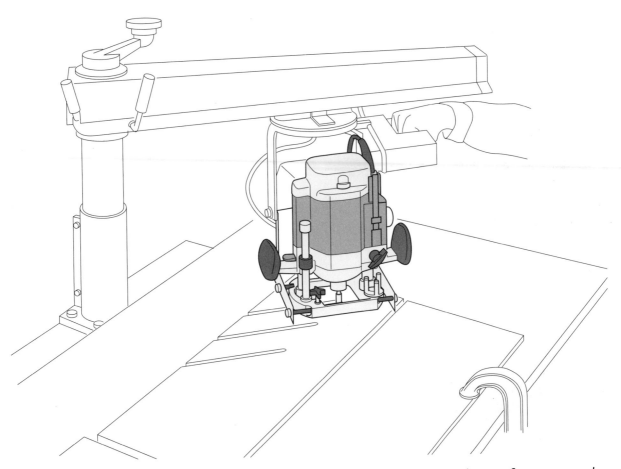

1–5. *Radial-arm saws, if fitted with an appropriate mounting plate to permit the attachment of a router, may be used for many routing applications. In most cases, this means removal of the sawing head before mounting the router. Some planning of the machining sequence is therefore essential to avoid repeated dismantling/assembly.*

manipulate the workpiece instead. Multi-purpose machines are available, such as certain radial-arm saws, to which the router may be attached or fixed temporarily, allowing it to be used at angles other than 90 degrees (1–5). Depending on the adaptability of the associated equipment, some variations on these modes are possible.

Most routers have a nominally circular base, in the center of which rotates the spindle, protruding from the motor housing. (Refer to Base on page 23 for more information on bases.) The spindle incorporates a collet, or chuck (described on pages 30 and 31), that is used to hold the rotary cutters, sometimes called "bits." During hand-routing operations, the machine is supported by the base resting on the workpiece, or sometimes on a template or guide. The distance between the motor and the base is adjustable to vary the cutter's depth of incision.

Types of Router

Two basic types of router are available: fixed-base (1–6) and plunge (1–7). As the names suggest, the base on the fixed type is not adjustable for depth of cut during the routing operation, but has to be fixed to hold the cutter at a prede-

1–6. *A mid-range, 1.5-horsepower fixed-base router with one speed of 25,000 rpm (revolutions per minute).*

1–7. *A typical heavy-duty 3.5-horsepower plunge router, capable of speeds from 8,000 to 20,000 rpm with electronic speed control.*

termined depth before routing commences. Plunge routers feature a spring-loaded arrange-

ment allowing vertical sliding of the motor housing on two pillars to vary the depth of cut during the routing operation. Preset stops can be engaged progressively to limit the depth of spindle travel (1–8). Some fixed-base models have the facility to detach the motor completely, allowing it to be attached to other apparatus, some of these dedicated to special applications. Thoughtful machine designers combine a scale fitted to the apparatus in order to allow immediate visual reference to the cutting depth (1–9).

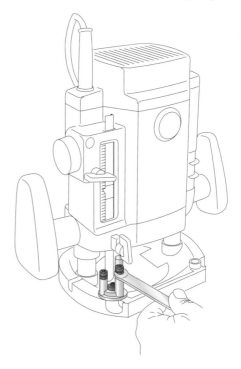

1–8. *Tightening turret-stop columns with a small wrench, or spanner, after setting the required height.*

Normally, in its role as a freehand woodworking tool, the router is controlled by gripping its two handles, which are located one either side of the motor housing (1–10). In the case of the plunge router, the handles may incorporate a locking function achieved by twisting or rotating, permitting the spindle depth to be fixed temporarily or, conversely, released (1–11). A variation preferred by some operators is a single D-handle

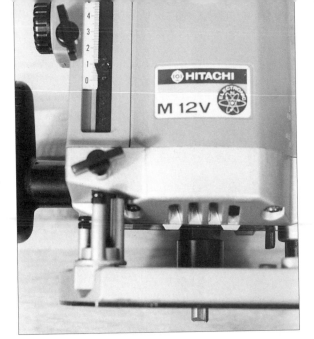

1–9. *The scale and pointer on this plunge router refer to the position of the motor housing and also, therefore, to the cutter depth. Before commencing a plunge cut, the scale may be adjusted to show zero and therefore indicate the depth of cut at any point to which the cutter is plunged.*

1–10. *Handles are usually designed for comfortable gripping and arranged for optimum control to facilitate secure freehand applications.*

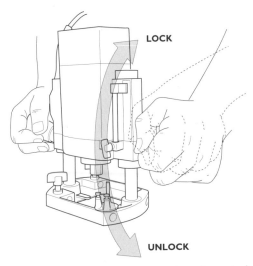

1–11. *Twisting of the wrist operates the column-locking device incorporated in the handle of this router.*

1–12. *A fixed-base router with a D-shaped handle, providing good directional control and an easy grip with a power switch incorporated in the handle.*

1–13. *In this example, the power switch requires a sliding action to activate it. A one-finger operation can be achieved without removing the grip from the handle.*

attached to one side of the router and incorporating an on-off switch (1–12). On-off switches are usually positioned close to the handles, permitting machine activation without loss of manual contact (1–13); this is not merely for convenience, but also for reasons of safety. (For more information about handles, refer to Handles, Locks, and Switches on pages 23 to 27.)

POWER CORD

DEPTH-
ADJUSTMENT
RING

HANDLE

COLLET AND NUT

MOTOR UNIT

SPINDLE LOCK

BASE

1–14. *A light-duty, 1-horsepower, fixed-base router with one speed: 25,000 rpm. It features a calibrated depth-adjustment ring.*

Motor power varies from as little as ¾ to as much as 3½ horsepower (about 550 to 2,500 watts). This is discussed further in Power on pages 21 and 22.

In order to evaluate the respective merits of both types of router, the following sections consider them separately.

FIXED-BASE ROUTERS

Fixed-base routers (1–14) were the first routers. They usually featured a detachable motor unit. Many accessories such as tables and special bases have become available to adapt fixed-base routers for special tasks. This is an advantage over the plunging router, which has a motor that is not normally detachable.

Adjustment of the depth of cut is by movement of the motor relative to the base (1–15), and several methods may be used to achieve this. One of the most fundamental types uses a base with a threaded sleeve into which the motor fits with a matching thread, similar to a large nut and bolt. Rotation of the two parts brings about depth

1–15. *With a fixed-base router, once set, the depth of cut remains constant during the routing. Fixed-base routers are fine for general handheld use, routing edges, template-guided work, and applications using jigs.*

adjustment on an infinitely variable micrometer principle. Other ways, such as a rack-and-pinion arrangement or a sliding sleeve, permit the adjustment of the cutter depth.

The base itself, usually circular, may vary in

LOCKING LEVER

ON-OFF SWITCH

HANDLE

DEPTH-STOP BAR

BASE

POWER CORD

DEPTH-ADJUSTMENT KNOB

ROTARY TURRETS

VERTICAL ADJUSTMENT SCREW

COLLET AND NUT

BASE

1–16. With a plunge depth of nearly 2½ inches, this heavy-duty router has a spindle capable of holding collet diameters of ¼, ⅜, and ½ inch.

design from one manufacturer to another but, ideally, is provided with sufficient apertures to provide visual contact with the cutter during routing operations.

PLUNGE ROUTERS

Identifiable by its two pillars—one either side of the machine—the plunge router (1–16) has the advantage of allowing adjustment of the cutting depth without interrupting the routing operation. It may be fixed at a chosen depth in a way similar to the fixed-base router (1–17), most often if it is connected to a table or bracket. Once the router is fitted to an accessory, the plunging feature may be utilized for depth adjustment.

Handles on the side of the machine are used for directional control in manual applications, and they usually feature a device for locking the motor housing at any given position to suit a particular depth of cut. Adjustment is simply a

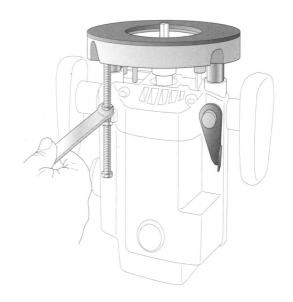

1–17. Some routers feature this device that allows the router to be fixed at a particular position by locking the housing with a locknut arrangement on a threaded column. This turns the plunge router into a fixed-base router.

matter of releasing the lock lever and then either bearing against the springs to increase the cutter depth or allowing the springs to push back the housing to decrease it. Once the required position has been achieved, it may be fixed by clamping with the lock lever (1–18 and 1–19). A lightweight machine in manual mode allows the facility to plunge the cutter into the workpiece and retract it when the cut is completed. (For more information about this, refer to Handles, Locks, and Switches on pages 23 to 27.)

Features

CAPACITIES AND DIMENSIONS

The charts on pages 155 to 158 summarize the capacities and dimensions of the range of routers

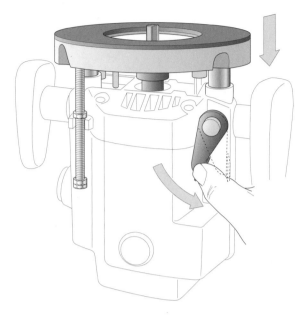

1–19. *Pressing down on the base of a plunge router to achieve a particular depth setting may be done manually; then the locking lever may be activated to fix the cutter at that depth.*

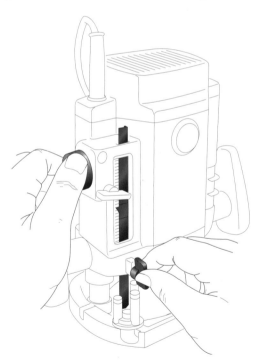

1–18. *Depth-setting device on a plunge router. Fine control is available by the rack adjuster, operated by rotating the knob on the side of the housing. The cutting depth is fixed securely with the locking screw on the front of the housing.*

ADVANTAGES AND DISADVANTAGES OF FIXED-BASE AND PLUNGE ROUTERS

It is true to say that both fixed-base and plunge routers have their respective merits. Because fixed-base routers generally have a detachable motor unit, they, unlike plunge routers, can be adapted for many special tasks with the use of accessories such as tables and special bases. A plunge router has an advantage in that its cutting depth can be adjusted without interrupting the router operation. And since the latter can function as a fixed type and generally comes with variable speed, it is gradually becoming the more popular. In fact, in Europe it is currently almost impossible to purchase a fixed-base model.

available currently. They are intended to be a general guide to show the major differences and help in choosing a router appropriate to an individual woodworker's needs. Some exceptions to the list exist, and the prospective owner is advised to examine the specifications of any machine to assess its suitability before purchasing it.

POWER AND SPEEDS

Power

In considering the router and, more accurately, the motor that is driving it, "power" means the available potential capacity, expressed in horsepower or watts. Horsepower (hp) is a practical term describing the amount of physical energy used, whereas watts are units of electrical activity. One horsepower is equal to 746 watts. Both terms are used by manufacturers in the specifications of their motorized products.

It is obvious that the greater the horsepower or wattage, the more powerful the motor. Routers may be fitted with motors as small as 1 horsepower to as great as 3½ horsepower, with a corresponding weight differential (1–20). Logically, the smaller machines being lighter and less powerful lend themselves more practically to handheld applications, such as edge-trimming, small-section molding, and template work. Weights of 5 to 8 pounds (about 2¼ to 3½ kilograms) for routers up to 1¾ hp are reasonable for manual applications, whereas the larger machines weigh in at about twice that of their smaller cousins.

1–20. *Two routers from the same manufacturer as examples of the two popular power sizes. On the left, a router with 3½ horsepower; on the right, one with 2 horsepower. Respective weights are 11.7 and 6.4 lbs.*

More powerful routers, capable of machining larger sections, are at their best when housed in a router table or other attachment that allows the use of hefty cutters (1–21). Dovetailing, shaping joinery components, and repetition milling are best done with a router of 2 hp or more. Smaller machines may be used for heavy work occasionally, but with discretion and care taken to avoid overloading the motor. Likewise, large machines may be applied to lightweight operations by using a smaller collet to accommodate a cutter with a smaller shank. (Refer to Collets on pages 30 to 32.) Certainly if a wide range of machining is to be undertaken in large volume and the available budget is sufficient, it is best to acquire at least one of each capacity.

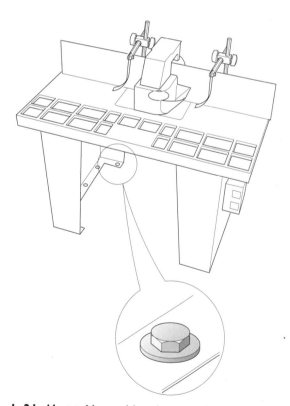

1–21. Most tables and benches intended for router attachment may be bolted to the ground or, if bench-top models (as shown here), may be attached to a sub-table.

Speeds

A great many of the fixed-base routers have only one speed, although most of the plunge machines currently available are equipped with multi-speed drives controlled by electronics. Clearly, the latter are more flexible and have more potential in terms of machining principles. (Refer to Routing Speeds on pages 95 and 96 for more information on methods and principles for applying different speeds.)

At least one router, a 1-hp model, rotates at 30,000 revolutions per minute (rpm); such a rate excludes all but the smallest-diameter cutters, if quality and safety are valued by the user. Usually, a single-speed model will rotate at around 25,000 rpm, but perfectly satisfactory operations are possible with speeds of 20,000 rpm or even less. Much depends on the size of the cutter and the depth of cut to which it is to be subjected. Within limits, one may assume that the faster the cut, the better will be the finish. Even so, the rate of feed plays a part in balancing the complex formula for optimum performance. The rate of feed is the speed at which the cutter is pushed into the workpiece, or the speed at which it is traversed along an edge. (This is also dealt with in Routing Speeds on pages 95 and 96.)

If a wide range of cutter diameters are planned, then it makes sense to use a router with variable speeds. Of these, the ones with electronic controls are the most practical (1–22).

Components

The router has several major components (1–23). These are the base, the handles, locks, and switches, the rotary turrets, and the collet. Each is discussed below.

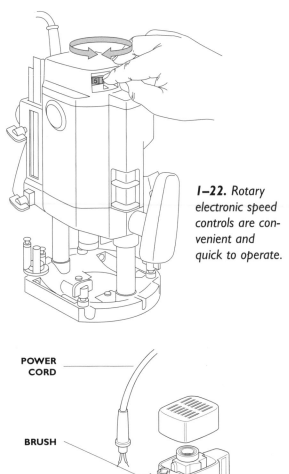

1–22. *Rotary electronic speed controls are convenient and quick to operate.*

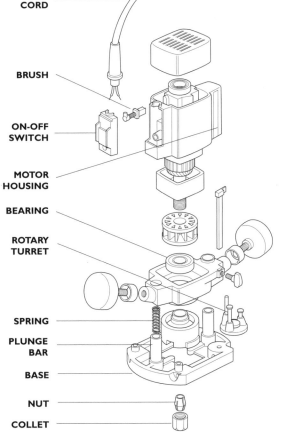

POWER CORD

BRUSH

ON-OFF SWITCH

MOTOR HOUSING

BEARING

ROTARY TURRET

SPRING

PLUNGE BAR

BASE

NUT

COLLET

1–23. *The parts of a router. Each of these parts is discussed in the following pages.*

BASE

The base is the contact between the router and the work surface. (Refer to 1–23.) It supports the motor unit either by direct connection, in the case of the fixed router, or by two bars in the case of the plunge router. Most bases are circular with at least one flat side, but there are variations on this basic shape.

In the center of the router base is a hole through which the spindle protrudes, allowing the attachment of cutters. It is common practice to attach a sub-base to the router for special applications, such as to increase the size of the base or to attach it temporarily to a bench. Usually, two fence bars are incorporated in the design of the base for the attachment of a fence, adjustable for distance from the cutter. This is generally for freehand routing and it is removable for other applications.

Refer to pages 33 and 34 for information on base maintenance techniques.

HANDLES, LOCKS, AND SWITCHES

These components are presented together in this chapter because, on the router, their operations are often combined.

Handles—normally two to a router—arranged one on each side, may simply be handgrips used to steer the router during manually guided operations. They vary in size, shape, and location according to the make (1–24 and 1–25). Whether they are situated near the base or higher up on the motor housing plays a part in the manipulation of the router, and individual applications vary as do router users. While the low position gives a good sense of control for freehand work, the handles may be impeded by templates and jigs. Handles located higher on the motor housing do not always feel as secure, but

HANDLE OVERVIEW

1–24 (top) and 1–25 (center). *Designs and locations of handles can differ greatly from model to model. It is advisable to handle various models before making a final choice. Even so, most routers can become familiar to the user with some practice.*

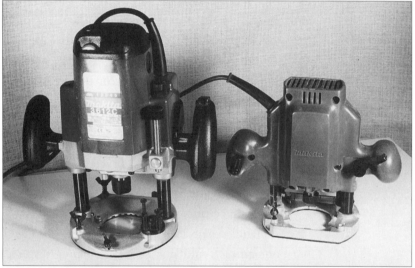

1–25.

1–26. *In this example, operation of the plunge-locking device is accomplished by the thumb.*

(continued on following page)

HANDLE OVERVIEW (CONTINUED)

1–27. A switch/handle combination. The fingers operate the power switch by gripping it, but as a safety precaution, the switch cannot be activated without first depressing with the thumb the button on top of the handle.

1–28. Without releasing the grip on the left-hand handle, the thumb can reach the sliding on-off switch to power the router.

are less likely to foul a template. A hands-on demonstration goes a long way in helping a prospective purchaser make a choice.

Other types of handle incorporate a locking mechanism to secure the motor position on a plunge router (1–26). There are also some handles that include an on-off power switch (1–27 and 1–28). Another design uses just one grip, called a D-handle. This is used exclusively with fixed-base routers.

It is not uncommon to come across a design of handle that may have angular adjustment, allowing changes to be made to suit individual users (1–29 to 1–31). This feature is particularly attractive to those who choose to use the router manually, but it is less useful to the user who combines the machine with a router table or similar attachment.

In the case of the plunge router, the handles do more than facilitate the steering of the machine; they also allow the hands to adjust the height of the motor and, therefore, the depth of cut dur-ing the progress of the routing operation. Suffi-cient downward pressure of the hands will over-come the spring-loaded pillars, bringing the motor closer to the workpiece. Easing of the pressure allows the spring to return the motor. At this point, it is worth mentioning the benefit of having the plunge lock mounted near a thumb or finger, to permit its activation with little movement of the hand. Thus, if it becomes nec-essary to plunge or raise the cutter during the routing operation, or to secure the particular depth of cut, it may be achieved without releas-

CHANGING HANDLE ANGLES

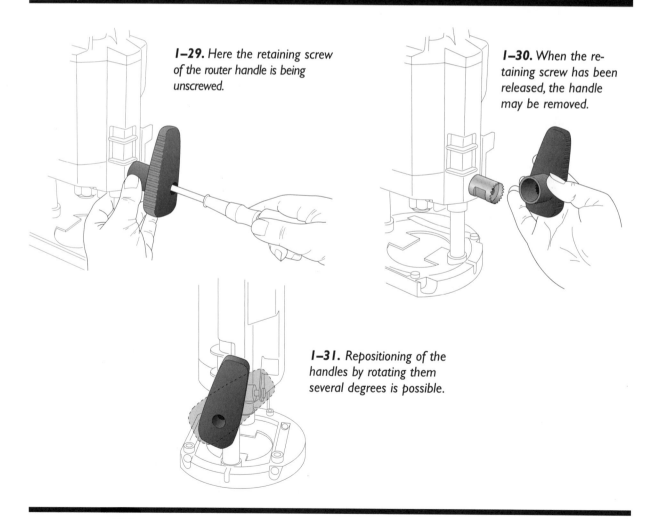

1–29. Here the retaining screw of the router handle is being unscrewed.

1–30. When the re-taining screw has been released, the handle may be removed.

1–31. Repositioning of the handles by rotating them several degrees is possible.

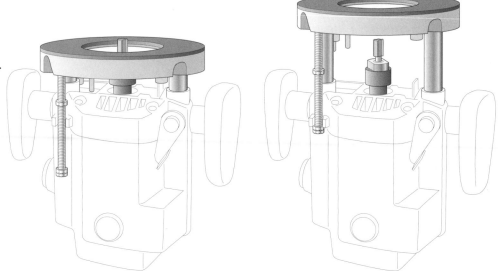

1–32 (left) and 1–33 (right). *After an operation requiring the projection of the cutter has been finished, the plunge router may be set aside with the cutter with-drawn for safety, as shown on the right.*

ing the grip on the handles. This is a facility that is not only efficient but safe.

Plunge routers have another safety benefit. When the router is set aside after an operation has been finished, the locking mechanism can be released and the motor house raised. This brings the cutter above the base plate, out of harm's way (1–32 and 1–33).

PLUNGE LOCKS

Plunge routers use plunge locks to fix the position of the motor that slides up and down on the columns; these are sometimes referred to as plunge bars. Sliding the motor is the means of controlling the depth of cut, because the cutter is held in the collet, which is, effectively, an extension of the motor spindle. Several facilities are available because of this function (1–34). Cutters may be entered, while revolving, into a workpiece by sliding the motor housing downwards until a preset stop is reached, and then fixed or locked at that depth by applying the plunge lock. Alternatively, the plunge lock may

be applied to hold the cutter at a preset depth and the router then applied as a fixed-base type.

The lock may be applied at any time and at any position within the router motor's range of movement.

Location of the locking mechanism and its mode of activation may vary widely, depending

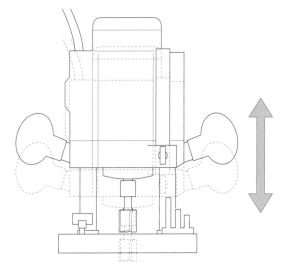

1–34. Plunge routers allow vertical movement to be carried out during routing operations, and some incorporate a locking mechanism in the handgrips that permits temporary locking of the cutting depth.

OPERATING LOCK LEVERS

 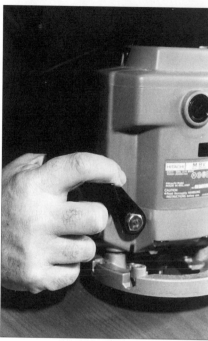 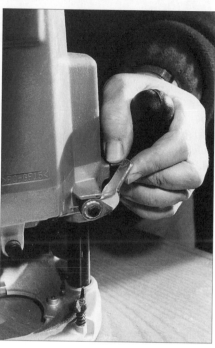

1–35 to 1–37. Some disciplined study should be applied to the operation of the locks and switches, as to whether it is more convenient to use thumb or fingers. Familiarity helps to build security (rather than contempt).

on the individual design. For example, some routers may have a rare locking function that is applied by twisting one of the two steering handles, making it a very convenient operation without disturbing the manual control of the machine. Others may have a separate locking lever, or trigger, near the handgrips but incorporated in the motor housing. These are of two types: those whose levers are pressed and those whose levers are raised to operate the lock. Another variation is a spring-release handle that applies the lock when it is released.

Lock levers are usually somewhat shorter than might be expected for secure handling when applying locking force, but many do not need great effort to hold the lock firmly. Generally, decisions must be made as to whether to use a

thumb or finger to activate the mechanism, but whichever method is used, it is best to establish a secure habit that will become a reliable component of the router setup (1–35 to 1–37).

Some plunge routers also have a fine adjuster knob (1–38).

ROTARY TURRETS

Rotary turrets are a major feature in the system of depth control on plunge routers.

As the name suggests, the rotary turret has a circular base fixed by a spring-loaded pin in its center to allow it to rotate (1–39). The turret is located beneath the depth stop rod installed in the motor housing. Rotation of the turret brings one of the "stops"—usually three—in vertical

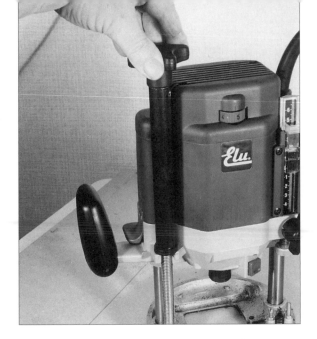

1–38. *Some routers may be provided with a fine adjuster, available as an accessory. Depth of cut is infinitely variable over the entire range of plunge movement.*

alignment with the depth-stop rod. Of the three stops, one is fixed and two are height-adjustable with screws and locknuts. Their function is to provide a staged depth setting to divide the cutting depth into two or three steps. For example, rather than strain the cutter, spindle, bearings, motor and, equally importantly, the operator, with a very deep cut of, say, 1½ inches, it may be achieved in three equal cuts of ½ inch. If a high-grade finish is needed, it is feasible to make a first cut ¾ inch deep, the second ⅝ inch, and the last, a "cleaning" cut, ⅛ inch (1–40).

An example of the practical application of the rotary turret is as follows: Having decided on the required depth of the cut, set the lowest tur-

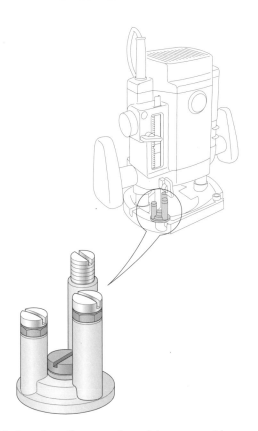

1–39. *A spring allows rotation of the turret without the need to release the retaining screw in the center of the turret base. Three columns may be preset to cover a range of cutting depths.*

1ST CUT — 3/4"

2ND CUT — 5/8"

3RD CUT — 1/8"

1–40. *Progressive cuts commencing with a coarse cut and finishing with a fine one will reduce strain on the cutter and bearings while ensuring a better finish on the machined workpiece.*

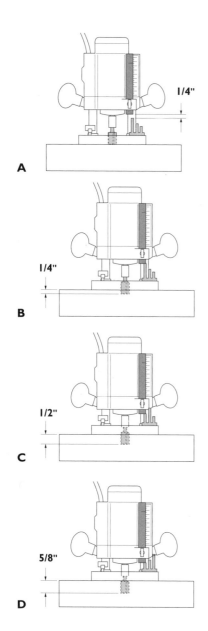

A

B

C

D

1–41. *A four-stage progressive operation to achieve a required depth using the presetting facility of the rotary turret. (A). Cutter is touching the workpiece and there is a gap of ¼ inch between the depth rod and the highest column on the rotary turret. (B). Thus, when the router is plunged to the first stop, the result is a ¼-inch-deep cut. (C). The router is raised and the turret is rotated to bring the next highest column under the depth rod; this allows the second cut to proceed, and the depth of cut is now increased to ½ inch. (D). For the final pass, the router is again raised and the turret rotated to align the lowest column with the depth rod. A cleaning cut of ⅛ inch brings the total depth to ⅝ inch.*

ret stop to that depth. The remaining two are set to divide the difference between the lowest point of the cut and the surface of the work-piece. All that is required then is to rotate the turret to align the appropriate stop with the depth stop rod (1–41).

Locknuts are used to fix or lock the adjusting screws inserted in the turrets to ensure security of the cutter depth during the routing operation and to enable repeat cuts to be made if necessary.

COLLETS

A collet resembles a miniature circular vise and is attached to the spindle of the router to hold the cutter. In principle, it is a hollow tapered cylinder with slots to allow its diameter to be reduced by external pressure, thus gripping the shank of the cutter (1–42). On the end of the router spindle a nut is screwed with a flanged end that engages the collet. This is the compression nut, and it is removed or slackened and the collet is inserted into the hollow spindle that is tapered to match the collet. When the nut is replaced and tight-ened onto the threaded spindle, the collet is forced into the tapered hole and is thus com-pressed. The internal diameter of the collet is very

1–42. *An assortment of split collets; some are single-, some double-, others multiple-split. Some require a com-pression nut, while others need only to be screwed into a spindle with a corresponding taper to produce the clamp-ing action.*

slightly larger than the shank of the cutter, so it needs very little closure to make a secure grip (1–43).

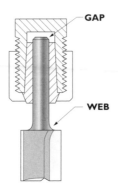

1–43. Diagram of a cutter installed correctly in the collet. Note: Most of the shank is inserted but not touching the extremity of the spindle aperture, and the web of the cutter body is not touching the collet jaws.

As with the collet, the collet gripping system must also be made to the most exacting manufacturing tolerances. It must not only be of the correct size but also be concentrically true in its internal and external diameters. Failure to meet this requirement would certainly mean inability of the cutter to perform properly, and, in all probability a disaster of a potentially dangerous kind could follow.

1–44. A simple spindle/cutter assembly using a grub screw to retain the cutter.

Collet Types

Considering the basic collet first, it is a straight sleeve into which the cutter shank is inserted and secured with a grub screw (1–44). This is fine until the thread has worn; then troubles develop in failing to secure the cutter. Only the cheapest models use this method and they are largely discontinued—with few regrets.

Currently, it is safe to assume that most collets will have one design feature in common: They will all have slits. The slit will run longitudinally along the length of the cutter, in some cases almost the whole length. Depending on the individual collet pattern, slits differ in number, from one to eight.

There is a type of collet that needs no compression nut, because it has an external thread to allow it to enter the spindle that is threaded to accept it (1–45). As the nut is screwed in tighter,

1–45. A tapered collet, needing no additional compression nut, with two inner sleeves to reduce collet diameter. Three diameters of cutter shank are applicable with this arrangement.

the tapered section of the collet meets the matching taper in the spindle, compression takes place and, consequently, the cutter is gripped (1–46 to 1–48).

Another design of collet—one of the type that use a compression nut—incorporates a self-release feature that, when it is unscrewed and the compression is released, the cutter is ejected. In recent versions of this variety, the nut and collet are supplied assembled and may not be separated, although the pair may be removed from the spindle as a unit.

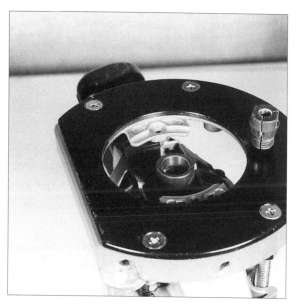

1–46. *A collet/spindle arrangement that requires no compression nut. The collet has a threaded end for assembly into the spindle.*

1–47. *Halfway down its body is a tapered section that matches the tapered internal diameter of the spindle.*

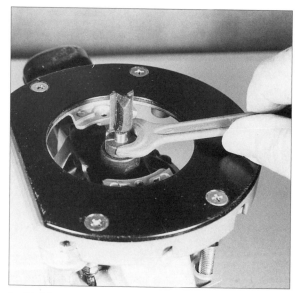

1–48. *The farther the collet is tightened into the spindle, the greater its diameter is reduced, thus gripping the cutter shank.*

Collet Sizes

Collets are referred to by the size of their internal, gripping diameter. In the United States, the common imperial sizes are ¼ and ½ inch. Also available are collets with ⅛- and ⅜-inch diameters, but these are less readily available and are usually associated with specialized cutters. In Europe there are approximate equivalents in metric sizes as well as accurate equivalents, all of which necessitates great care to establish with absolute certainty the diameter of both cutter and collet before trying to assemble them.

Here is a list of collet diameters in both imperial and metric sizes, arranged in size order:

3 mm
⅛ inch (3.2 mm)
6 mm
¼ inch (6.35 mm)
8 mm
⅜ inch (9.5 mm)
10 mm
12 mm
½ inch (12.7 mm)

Cutters and collets of metric diameters may

be interchanged with their imperial equivalents, but not otherwise. Doing so would cause distortion of the collet, with hazardous consequences.

Needless to say, it is essential that the diameters of the collet and cutter shank match; and, with regard to installation and removal, another important observation must be made: When installing the collet, especially a multi-segment type, it should be placed in its locking nut and centered before being fitted into the router spindle (1–49). This is to avoid the possibility of misalignment that could damage the assembly if pressure were to be applied by the retaining nut in this situation.

Router Care and Maintenance

Router owners who wish to prolong the useful life of their machines readily accept the need for careful maintenance checks. A regular program is advised, suitable for each user according to the amount of work that is being done by the particular machine. This is generally a question of applying "senses" in the true meaning of the word; that is, using sight, touch, smell, and hearing.

The enemies of good routing are primarily wear and waste, the latter attacking in the form of wood resin, grease, and dust particles, all of which may adhere to parts of the machine, which should be kept as clean as possible. This harmful debris is easily removed with the correct treatment—and this will be separately detailed below—but first, consider a checklist of the parts that need inspection.

The sequence proceeds from the bottom to the top of the router: base, plunge bars, collets, bearings, motor housing, switch gear, brushes, and power cable. Each is discussed below.

BASE

Because this is the most common point of contact between the router and the work surface, the base (1–50) should be clean and smooth. Often traces of resin or gum from wood may adhere to it; these must be removed to ensure free movement of the handheld

1–49. Here there are two sizes of collet applicable to the matching spindle. Two wrenches are required for this model, one to hold the spindle and the other to operate the compression nut.

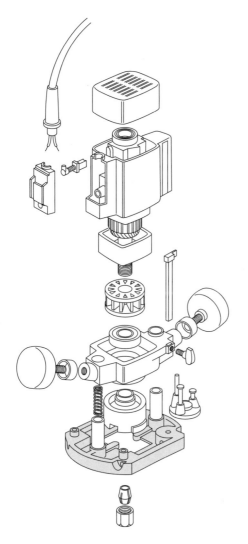

1–50. Router base.

router. Most sticky deposits may be removed by applying a solvent with a brush and wiping it off with a cloth. Deposits that are more stubborn may be eased off with a plastic scraper. Scratches are not uncommon and removing them should be handled with care, because any attempt to abrade the blemished area locally may deform the surface and even produce deeper scratches. This would only create a worse situation, so it is better to clean up the entire surface of the base with a fine abrasive paper laid on a flat surface. A badly

scored surface might be best treated by replacement with a new base plate.

An integrated function of most base plates is the housing of the fence bars—two aspects of which need attention. One is the smooth running of the rods in the base, and the other is the efficient operation of the screws used to secure the rods. Cleaning the bars with a stiff brush soaked in a grease solvent and then applying an oil-free lubricant of the silicon or PTFE variety should suffice. As to the securing screws; these lock the base to the fence bars by the application of pressure and, therefore, are a potential cause of damage. Normal finger tightness is usually enough to secure the base, without the need to resort to the use of pliers or wrenches. Even so, if the end of a screw is damaged or rough, it may mark the bar permanently. Inspection of the screw followed by some careful work with a file and abrasive paper if necessary should be an adequate preventative.

PLUNGE BARS

On routers that incorporate a plunging action, free movement of the motor/spindle system is only possible if the bars and sleeves are correctly aligned. If at any time the router is dropped, suspect that some damage may have occurred that might cause binding of these parts and inspect the movement of these parts thoroughly.

Not only does the plunge action allow entry of the cutter into the work while the router is running, but if the spring return is not locked, the cutter can be removed when manual pressure is released. This permits the router to be set aside with the cutter raised out of harm's way above the work surface.

In some cases, the return springs are enclosed within the plunge bars (1–51); in others, the spring is fitted externally. Either way, the springs work better if they are seated properly and cleaned regularly.

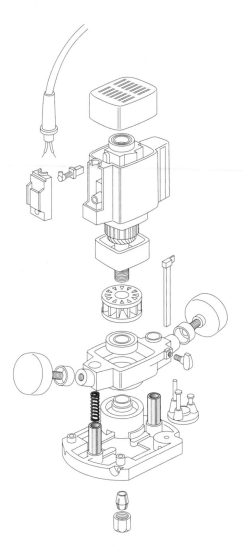

1–51. Plunge bars and return springs. The springs should be seated properly and regularly cleaned, and the plunge bars must also be cleaned regularly so that they run smoothly within their sleeves.

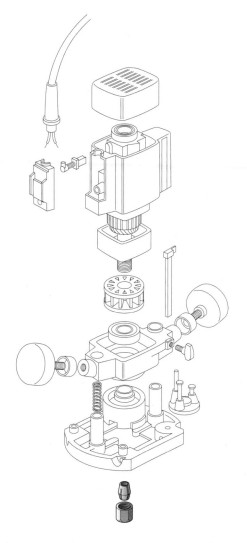

1–52. Collet and compression nut. The collet's slits and barrel must be cleaned regularly to ensure that the mating surfaces have proper contact.

The bars themselves must also be clean to ensure smooth running within their sleeves. Both the springs and bars can be cleaned by applying solvents to remove the resin deposits, followed by a light, dry lubricant.

Part of the plunge-action system is the locking mechanism with which the motor assembly is fixed at any point in its available travel. Only one part, the lever, moves on this mechanism and,

as with other parts, cleaning and lubricating is necessary.

COLLETS

Since the collet (1–52) is the contact between the router spindle and the cutter, it follows that every effort must be made to ensure that the collet is in perfect condition at all times. Whichever type of collet is fitted to the router, principles of care are universal. Regular inspection and cleaning of the slits and the barrel to remove resin is important, to prevent inadequate contact between the mating surfaces. If such a problem is not corrected, it becomes progressive, leading to ovality in the spindle/collet assembly and eccentricity in the revolution of the cutter. In particular, carefully examine for any debris that might adhere to the tapered surfaces, with special attention to the insides of the slits. Any waste matter clinging to the collet is a potential danger to correct seating and securing of the cutter.

It is possible that a particular router setup might be used with no need to remove the cutter or collet assembly for several days. Although there is very apt old saying, "If it ain't broke, don't fix it!", there are a few exceptions and this is one. After a sequence of machining operations when a hot router is set aside until, say, the next day, there is a possibility of condensation developing in or around the spindle assembly. This can lead to corrosion, with obvious undesirable consequences, possibly leading to fouling of the surfaces between the spindle, collet, and cutter. So, regular inspection followed by cleansing is recommended (1–53). A toothbrush dressed with light machine oil should be carefully applied; or, if residues are stubborn, a brass brush used for cleaning suede leather. But no coarse abrasives should be used for this purpose. Spray-on solvents are effective, but be careful not to direct the spray into a bearing guide if there is one fitted to the cutter, as this could dissolve its essential lubrication. Purposely made brass brushes, cylindrical in shape, are available for cleaning the collet bore. Before reassembly, the components should be wiped to remove any oil, no lubrication being necessary in the collet assembly; in fact, its presence would

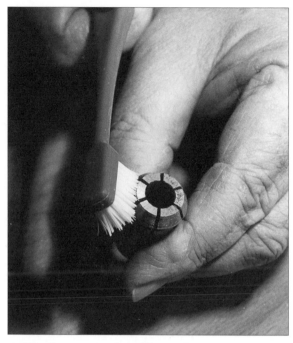

1–53. Cleaning a collet with a stiff toothbrush helps to remove debris from the surface and from inside the slits.

be detrimental because of its tendency to attract waste dust.

As the foregoing suggests, for the investment of a few minutes' diligence, it is a prudent habit to disassemble the collet/cutter components after each session for cleaning purposes. A light film of oil can be left on the surfaces as a corrosion inhibitor, until next time the router is used. Because there is a possibility of staining the workpiece, clean off any residual oil prior to applying the cutter.

BEARINGS

Bearings (1–54) are housed at the top and bottom of the shaft (spindle). They are usually of high-quality pilot-bearing (ball-race bearing) design and are expected to give excellent service, providing the router is not unduly abused. No maintenance measures are available directly to the user, but it is advised that the user listen to the sound of the rotating spindle. This can indicate the condition of a bearing. Under load, a worn bearing will be indicated by abnormal sounds (different sounds that occur suddenly or intermittently), and the operator should follow up with a secondary inspection. A worn or an asymmetrical cutter could be responsible for this condition, so, after disconnecting the power supply, examination of its cutting edge and its installation should be carried out before proceeding further.

If all appears to be well in respect to the cutter and its assembly, then the next step is to test the condition of the spindle housing. Pressure should be applied to the cutter, preferably with gloved hands, for safety. First, apply pressure from side to side, around an imaginary compass, that is, from north to south and from east to west, to test for any free movement. Similarly, the cutter may be pressed up and down with the fingers; be sensitive to any sign of play in the spindle. If any movement in either direction is detected, the likelihood is that wear is present in one or both bearings. A thorough inspection is recommended and this requires a complete dismantling of the router spindle assembly. Although modern ball bearings are extremely durable, faults can occur, and if replacement is necessary it is a job best handled by service engineers. The manufacturers or suppliers will most likely advise the nearest authorized service center, if the router needs specialist attention.

MOTOR HOUSING

Cutters have an abrading action at the same time as they cut or slice the work. This produces fine, powdery waste that clings to almost anything it touches. The router itself is the first line of contact, offering its crevices, cavities, and airways as targets. Most motor housings (1–55) have some, or all, of these built-in dust trays. Because of the need to supply a cooling flow of air to the motor, it is essential to keep clean all orifices that lead to the fan-assisted system incorporated in the motor housing.

It may be tempting to use compressed air to shift dust particles. In fact, it is not uncommon to hear of this practice being advocated by certain so-called "experts," but before using an air hose, consider this: Even a low-pressure air

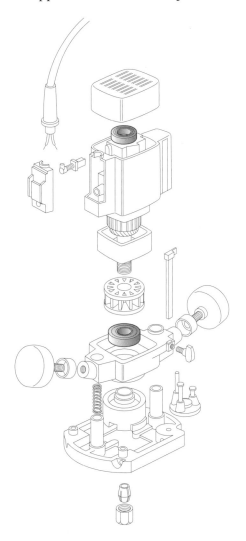

1–54. Spindle bearings.

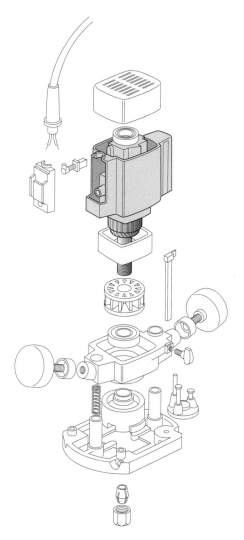

SWITCH GEAR

The cleaning methods used for the switch gear (1–56) are similar to those applied to the motor housing, previously detailed. Additionally, when the router is switched off and the power plug is removed from the electrical supply, it is a simple matter to disassemble the switch for better cleaning and inspection. Brass terminals, switch levers, springs, and contacts should all be cleaned and checked for wear, before reassembly.

1–55. Motor housing. The best way to clean the motor housing is to stir up the dust with a brush while vacuuming up the particles with a vacuum hose.

supply directed at a dust-laden area has sufficient force to drive the particles far into the machinery where they would be difficult to remove.

It is better to agitate the accumulated dust, with a brush, while bringing a vacuum hose near to draw off the disturbed particles. Any discarded brush will do, particularly those intended for paint; even toothbrushes are useful for accessing tight corners.

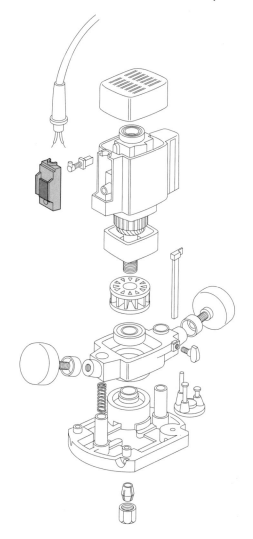

1–56. On-off switch. Use the cleaning methods for the motor housing on the switch gear, that is, a brush and a vacuum hose.

It is unnecessary to go to this trouble frequently, unless the router is used on a daily basis, and then a thorough program of maintenance about every two weeks should include all the points mentioned in this chapter.

BRUSHES

A gradually progressive sparking from the motor housing is probably an indication of the brushes wearing. Brushes (1–57) are usually accessible via their housings, which are incorporated in the motor casing. Refer to the manual supplied with the router to identify the plugs—there are normally two—that cover the brush holders. With the plugs removed, it is a simple matter to withdraw the brushes. To the inexperienced, the name "brush" may seem incorrect when seeing one for the first time, as there are no bristles associated with the component, it being a rectangular block of carbon. The name probably originates from the fact that the carbon block rubs against, or "brushes," the surface of the commutator—the segmented metal cylinder mounted on the armature shaft of the electric motor—as it revolves.

As the brushes wear, they may leave a deposit on the commutator, creating an inefficient contact; this deposit should be cleaned off. A fine abrasive paper may be applied gently to achieve this, but the accent is on the words "fine" and "gently"—the object being to clean away the deposit and not to damage the surface of the commutator.

In time the brushes may be worn away, necessitating replacement. Selection of the correct part is obvious, because various shapes and sizes may be offered. Having replaced the brushes, the operator may notice that for a short time there is evidence of sparking due to carbon dust

overheating and being discharged from the interior. This should gradually disappear as the carbon blocks wear away to the shape of the rotating commutator.

A word of caution in refitting of the plugs that cover the brushes: Make sure the brushes and springs are free to move in the housing and that the threaded plugs are fitted accurately without binding.

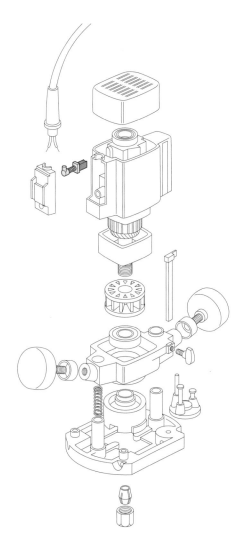

1–57. Carbon brush. Worn brushes leave a deposit on the commutator–the segmental metal cylinder mounted on the armature shaft of the motor—that can be gently removed with a fine abrasive paper.

POWER CABLE

Regular inspection is the order of the day with any power cable (1–58). Look especially at terminal points, where cables are fitted to plugs and switches; replace any cables or metal parts that have blue coloring indicating signs of burning (1–59). Thoughtful manufacturers fit rubber or plastic sleeves to protect cables at their entry into the motor housing. This is where most wear is likely, and if the power cable is not protected in this manner it is wise to add a sleeve by winding some insulating adhesive tape around the power cable. The same tape may be applied at any point on the cable where there might be some frequent abrasion due to negotiating a bend or cable tie.

On the rare occasion when it is required to replace the cable, the correct specifications must be observed, by reference to the manual and not merely by matching the one taken from the machine—in case it was already replaced by an incorrect type.

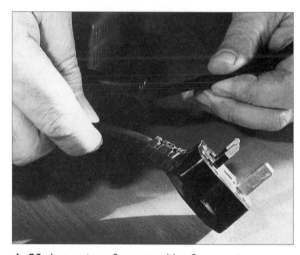

1–59. Inspection of power cables for wear is an essential part of maintenance. Unlike static machinery, power tools that are used in freehand operations are more likely to wear the cable due to frequent movement. Examine the whole cable, with special care for ends where cables enter motor housings or plugs.

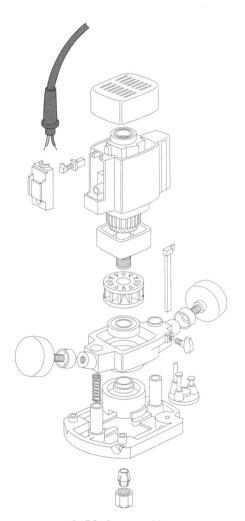

1–58. Power cable.

CHAPTER 2 Cutters

Solid-Steel and Carbide-Tipped Cutters

There are two general types of cutters: solid-steel and carbide-tipped.

Solid-steel cutters (2–1), whether they are made from carbon steel (CS) or high-speed steel (HSS), offer some advantages and disadvantages to the user over the carbide-tipped variety. The advantages are that they are less expensive and that, size for size, they are more easily sharpened with a hone. Used with softwoods and the less abrasive hardwoods, solid-steel cutters will give a respectable performance in terms of finish and durability. It is possible to produce a keener cutting edge on an HSS cutter than one of CS.

Cutters may also be made of solid tungsten carbide (STC). This material is usually limited to the manufacture of smaller-diameter cutters, the geometrical specifications of which are similar to the HSS variety.

Refer to Cutter Care on pages 59 to 64 for more information on solid-steel cutters.

Tungsten-carbide-tipped (TCT) cutters (2–2) are made from tungsten, a metal found chiefly in wolframite (a mineral that consists of tungstate of iron and manganese), which is combined with carbide to increase its durability. Design of the

2–1. Solid cutters are usually made from carbon steel or high-speed steel, and they are more easily sharpened with a hone than tungsten carbide-tipped cutters. It is possible to produce a keener cutting edge on an HSS cutter than one of CS.

2–2. Solid-tungsten carbide is sometimes used for the entire cutter rather than only as a cutting tip, as shown in these two examples.

tip and the material from which it is made are crucial to the cutter's performance, and to understand these elements thoroughly in order to better judge the cutter's quality, it is necessary to study them more closely.

Consider first the raw materials from which the cutter is made. Good-quality steel is essential for the body of the cutter, and the form should be machined from a solid drawn-steel bar rather than from cast steel. The latter is quicker and cheaper to produce, but makes an inferior tool. Cutter tips are ideally made of a high-grade carbide bonded by cobalt and tungsten. A uniform consistency of the materials, together with a fine grain, is essential to the durability and sharpness of the tip. A cheaper product may well have a coarse-grain material, which is likely to lead to early destruction of the sharp edge, thus requiring more frequent sharpening and giving a poorer performance.

Cutter Geometry

The geometry of the cutter is also crucial to the quality of the cutter's output. The following features are worth considering when choosing cutters: anti-kickback design, shear angle, radial relief, rake, clearance, and surface treatment. Each is described below.

ANTI-KICKBACK DESIGN

When the initial contact is made between the workpiece and the cutter, a "kickback" may occur. This tendency can be reduced by increasing the spread of the shoulders supporting the tips and thus reducing the initial depth of cut (2–3). Look for this in cutters ¾ inch in diameter or more.

SHEAR ANGLE

Cutting edges are set at a shear angle of zero, positive, or negative. Viewing the cutter with the tips up and the shank down, look at the width of the tips to see if their cutting edges are straight up or down (zero shear), slanting down from right to left (positive shear), or slanting down from left to right (negative shear, as shown in 2–4).

The angle of shear is responsible for the behavior of the cutter and the way it performs. An angled shear is generally better than a straight, or zero, shear, because there is more contact during the cutting operation, producing therefore a smoother cut. Of the two angled types, the negative shear is preferable for use where an especially clean finish is needed, as in laminate trimming.

RADIAL RELIEF

Radial relief is the amount of clearance behind the cutting edge to prevent friction between the bit and the cut surface (2–5). It may be a straight angular clearance or, better, a radiused clearance that gives more support to the tip when it is under duress. The extra mass supporting the tip clearly gives several advantages over the straight-angled clearance: It strengthens the edge, keeps the edge sharper longer, meaning less maintenance and more economy, and reduces burning and chattering. The degree by which the clearance leaves the tip is called the cutting angle.

RAKE ANGLE

The rake, or hook, angle is the angle made by the face of the tip to the centerline of the cutter body. (Refer to 2–5.)

CUTTER GEOMETRY

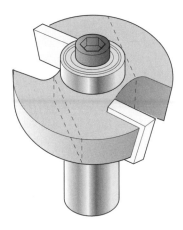

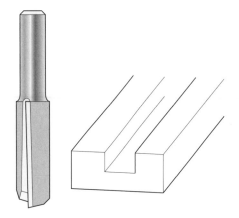

2–3. *Well-spread shoulders behind the cutting tips help to prevent kickback in routing applications. Notice how much less would be the support if the shoulders were reduced in spread as shown by the dotted lines.*

2–4. *An example of downward cutting with a negative-shear cutter. Clean, smooth cutting is available with this type of cutter.*

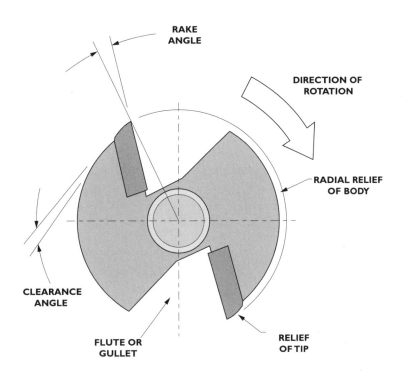

2–5. *Desirable features on a well-designed two-flute cutter.*

(continued on following page)

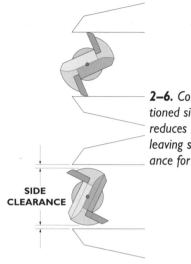

2–6. *Correctly proportioned side clearance reduces friction while leaving sufficient clearance for chip ejection.*

SIDE CLEARANCE

2–7. *To help reduce the tendency to collect resinous debris, the body of the cutter should be coated with a non-stick material. Shown here is a fine example of a large-diameter, bearing-guided, panel raiser.*

SIDE CLEARANCE

Side clearance is the difference between the diameter of the tip and the cutter body (2–6). Clearance is necessary to avoid friction between the body and the cut surface and also to give clearance to the waste created by the cutting action.

SURFACE TREATMENT

An important feature of the finish given to the body of the cutter is the surface treatment (2–7). Ideally, a coating of a non-stick material will have been deposited on the body, not the cutting tip. This is to reduce the tendency of the body to collect resins and other residues generated by the cutting action.

Cutters made from HSS are not usually coated, because they are machined from one solid bar and are entirely highly polished.

Selecting Cutters

Deciding whether to use HSS or TCT cutters depends largely on whether one uses mainly wood or man-made boards. For wood, HSS is fine unless the lumber is unusually hard or selected (a term used to describe highest-quality lumber).

When choosing cutters, it is best to examine them if possible, to ascertain by eye if they are of acceptable quality. This should be done as a matter of safety as much as for performance, because cutters may be damaged, even if they have been made correctly.

When examining a cutter, its shank, tip design, and tip brazing should be considered. Each of these features is discussed below.

SHANK

It is not possible to check, without some very accurate measuring equipment, the concentricity of the shank relative to the cutter tips; this is a feature that must initially be taken for granted. It is possible, however, to examine the surface for flaws (2–8). If the surface is polished correctly,

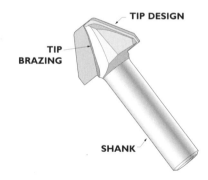

TIP DESIGN

TIP BRAZING

SHANK

2–8. *When cutters are being purchased, the quality of the cutter shank and the design of the tip should be noted. At the same time, the quality of the brazing between the tip and the cutter body should be inspected. Any flaws in any of these main features means rejection of the cutter.*

even the slightest blemish is detectable, by naked eye or with a magnifying lens. A cutter with a visible fault should be rejected because the potential damage to the workpiece, collet, and router—not to mention the operator—may be far more than the cost of the cutter. The shank should be smoothly chamfered at the end to aid its insertion into the collet.

TIP DESIGN

If you are choosing a cutter for a plunge router, see that the tips extend beyond the end of the cutter body in order that the plunging process can be achieved. For the same reason, the ends of the tips should be "backed off" at an angle to allow chip clearance (2–9).

View the cutter from the side to assess whether the shear angle is zero, positive, or negative and choose according to the type of work to be undertaken (2–10).

2–10. Sometimes it is necessary to trim boards with both surfaces laminated. For this purpose the cutter illustrated is used. Note that the upper and lower blades are arranged respectively in negative and positive shear to cut cleanly and simultaneously the laminated edges on each side of the board.

TIP BRAZING

In the case of TCT cutters, examine the brazing of the tip to the body and see that it is a clean, unbroken line. This is obviously not as good as a laboratory test, but it is better than accepting the cutter without looking at it.

Buying Cutters

It is worthwhile to acquire catalogs from the cutter manufacturers to ascertain which will suit the requirements of the individual user. An amazing variety awaits the newcomer to routing, choosing from which is sufficient to fill many a winter's evening (2–11). Finally, if it is not possible to shop around from a selection of stores to inspect the products before buying, purchase the cutters from a reputable dealer by mail order, preferably a company with the confidence in its products to offer a no-quibble replacement in the case of a genuine complaint.

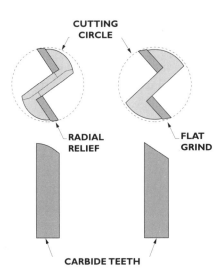

CUTTING CIRCLE

RADIAL RELIEF

FLAT GRIND

CARBIDE TEETH

2–9. Viewed end-on, the cutting edges may be seen to be "backed off," giving either a radiused or straight relief. It's better if this relieved profile is radiused, because this supports the cutting edge better, with reduced tendency to chip.

2–11. *A selection of the almost inexhaustible range of shapes that can be made with the cutters currently available from manufacturers. The three profiles at the bottom of the illustration are examples of how composite shapes may be customized by applying successive passes with standard cutters.*

Types of Cutter

STRAIGHT CUTTERS

Straight cutters, as the name implies, have straight cutting edges and parallel flutes (2–12). Many applications are available with straight cutters, including cutting grooves, dadoes (or channels), slots, mortises, recesses, and removing waste. With the use of an appropriate fencing system, other applications, such as beveling or angle cutting, are possible.

There are several versions of this type of cutter with multiple flutes, though the most popular are single- or double-fluted. Both are described below.

As mentioned in the section Cutter Geometry on pages 42 to 44, the straight cutter's edges may be set at a shear angle of zero, positive, or negative.

Straight cutters are good for straight grooving with a side fence or for following a template guide. If the cutter is not fitted with a self-guiding bearing, it can be used with a guide-bush system (2–13), more information about which is detailed in Guide Bushes on pages 111 to 113.

In plunging operations with straight cutters, it is wise to limit the depth of cut to a maximum of ³⁄₁₆ inch (5 mm) in order to reduce the risk of overheating. Any depths more than this should be achieved in a series of shallow steps. (Refer to 1–40 on page 29.)

Single-Flute Cutters

A single flute means a single cutting edge; this allows for fast routing with plenty of chip clear-

2–12. *A standard straight-flute router cutter. It could be solid steel or carbide-tipped.*

2–13. *For use with templates or jigs, routers may be guided by bushings that are attached to the router base. Many diameters are available offering flexibility of application. Refer to Chapters 7 and 9 for more information on template and jig use.*

ance (2–14). The end result is high productivity, but not a high-class finish. Single-flute cutters are excellent for roughing out a blank workpiece in preparation for template work. (Refer to Templates on pages 109 to 114 for more details.) Good for plunge-cutting, boring holes, etc., they are available mainly in small diameters.

Double-Flute Cutters

Double-flute cutters have two cutting edges (2–15). Having two blades means twice as many cutting strokes per minute than the single-flute cutter; therefore, the surface left by the cutting action is cleaner. In addition to the side-cutting function—providing that the cutter ends are extended beyond the body—this cutter is useful for many types of work, including plunge routing. The facility to cut at the very end of the cutter makes it useful for "bottoming" grooves and similar operations.

Three-Flute Cutters

Three-flute cutters (refer to 2–15) are excellent for fine finishes for trimming work and are often available in larger diameters where the gullets are less likely to jam the shavings.

Multi-Flute Cutters

Multi-flute cutters (refer to 2–15) are made to be used at low speeds, because their smaller flutes have reduced waste clearance and this increases the possibility of overheating. Cutters can have 12 or more flutes, and this type should be regarded as a rotary rasp, intended for applications similar to grinding or abrading and applied accordingly.

Spiral-Flute Cutters

The spiral form of the straight cutter (2–16) is intended for a wide variety of applications but

CUTTER FLUTES

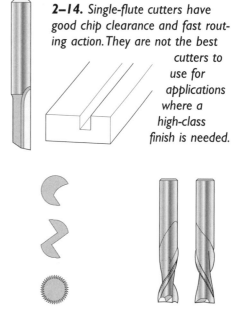

2–14. *Single-flute cutters have good chip clearance and fast routing action. They are not the best cutters to use for applications where a high-class finish is needed.*

2–15. *End views of cutters. Top, single-flute; center, two-flute; bottom, multi-flute, or burr.*

2–16. *For the severing, trimming, and pattern-copying of laminated panels this spiral-fluted cutter is ideal.*

especially for severing panels as well as copying and cutting them to a predetermined size with templates or other guiding systems. Spiral-flute cutters are applicable for laminates and plastics and for most solid-wood projects.

SELF-GUIDING CUTTERS

Developed to produce copies from a template, or pattern, the self-guiding cutter (2–17) relies on making contact with the template while revolving and cutting simultaneously. The bearing acts like a fence—in other words, producing a predetermined width of cut, depending on the difference between the diameter of the bearing and the cutter.

A bearing may be one of two types: the pin-ended variety (2–18), machined from the solid body of the cutter, and those with a pilot (ball-race bearing) that is fitted separately to the shank of the cutter (2–19).

Cutters with pin-end bearings are less expensive but less efficient, with a great tendency to leave burn marks on wood workpieces. This is hardly surprising, because the pin end is rubbing directly against the work and acting as a revolving fence. In any operation with a pin-end bearing, as slow as possible is the best advice for the motor speed, and there should be no more sideways pressure than is necessary on the template or workpiece when routing.

The pilot bearing (or ball bearing) is a device comprising two circular bearing wheels between which run steel balls that allow the inner and outer wheels to turn while they are under load. This means that if in a routing application the outer, guiding, wheel, were to meet some obstruction or be stopped for any reason, the cutter could still run freely within the bearing.

When pilot or ball bearings are fitted to cutters, they are usually attached to the shaft of the cutter,

SELF-GUIDING CUTTERS

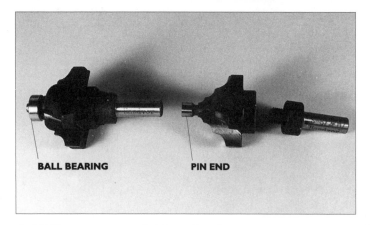

BALL BEARING   PIN END

2–17. Two cutters intended for self-guiding operations with end-bearings; the left one has a ball bearing and the right a solid pin end. The former is clearly more efficient because it runs freely when in contact with the workpiece or template, while the latter has a tendency to leave a mark due to the friction its contact creates.

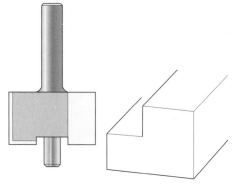

2–18. Pin-ended bearings are so-called because of the solid bearing extended from the end of the cutter. Caution is called for in the application of this cutter with pin-ended bearings, for excessive side force will cause burning and scarring of the workpiece from friction (caused by the bearing contact).

(continued on following page)

either below (that is at the end of the cutter) or above it (2–20). Cutter shafts are reduced in diameter to accommodate the bearings and, in the case of those fitted on the end of the shaft, a screw enters a threaded hole in the shaft center and its head retains the bearing. This is the type of bearing arrangement that is most commonly in use.

Ball bearings that are fitted on the shank above the cutter are retained by a collar that incorporates a grub screw which is tightened with an Allen or hexagon wrench. They are especially useful for trimming and are applied where a template is positioned above the work.

The outside diameter of a bearing may be increased by adding an outer ring of plastic or metal. This creates a greater difference in the diameters of the bearing and the cutter, resulting in a different width of cut. It is possible to purchase outer rings of various diameters for this purpose, enabling quick changes to be made to the cut width without changing the basic setup. By using a graded selection of bearing diameters progressively, it is possible to create a range of stepped effects or decorative moldings with only one template arrangement on the same workpiece (2–21).

SELF-GUIDING CUTTERS (CONTINUED)

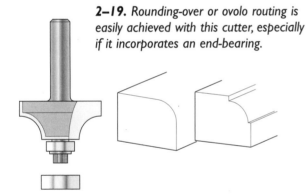

2–19. Rounding-over or ovolo routing is easily achieved with this cutter, especially if it incorporates an end-bearing.

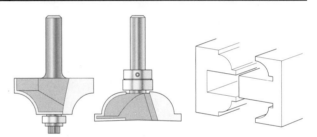

2–20. This ovolo set is used for profiling and scribing on the "cope- and- stick" principle to produce matching frame members. Note the bearings; one is shank-fitted, and the other is fitted on the end of the cutter.

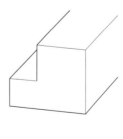

2–21. For rabbets (rebates) and corner recessing, this set of interchangeable bearings allows different depths of recess with one cutter.

SPECIAL-PURPOSE CUTTERS

Molding Cutters

Cutters designed for molding edges of frames, panels, and other members that require a decoration are available in a vast range of shapes and sizes (2–22 and 2–23). Some have a specific function as well as the potential for producing attractive profiles and sections. When these cut-

2–22. Largely used for decorating panel edges and other similar applications, molding cutters come in a vast range of shapes and sizes. They are usually found with end-bearings for self-guiding.

2–23. This set of cutters uses a shaft to which are attached pairs of cutters for the production of molded edges. Several different patterns may be fitted to the shaft; for safety, both matching cutters in the paired set must be attached.

ters are applied to panel edges or members of any size, it may be preferable to take the router to the workpiece. For the production of small strip items, such as attachable moldings, a fixed router installed in a table or overhead bracket will be more practical.

Profile Scribers

A desirable combination of ornamentation and function is achievable with these cutters (2–24). A basic requirement of conventional cabinet

2–24. Profile-scribing cutters are designed to produce scribed joints, especially the cope-and-stick (stile-and-rail) joints found largely in small frames. Two cutters are assembled on the shaft in two positions to produce both of the required elements of the joint.

doors is that their framing is grooved to hold an internal panel. They are normally decorated with a molding, and their construction requires that the four sides be joined by mortise-and-tenon joints. By assembling the components of a set of scribing cutters and groovers to form a simple pattern, it is possible to produce the panel groove, a decorative molding, and the joint—all from the same set (2–25).

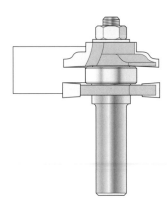

2–25. *Between the two profile scribers is the bearing against which the outer edge of the workpiece will be guided. After routing the frame sides, the cutters are disassembled and remounted to produce matching frame ends. Another cope-and-stick application, but with an economical cutter system.*

Panel-Raising Cutters

Produced for "raising," or "fielding," panels, these cutters are used to reduce the edge of a panel to the thickness required for insertion into the grooved frame of a cabinet door (2–26 and 2–27).

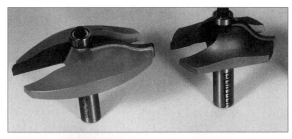

2–26. *"Raised," or "fielded," panels are created with the help of these cutters. They are usually combined with profile scribers in the production of framed-paneled doors.*

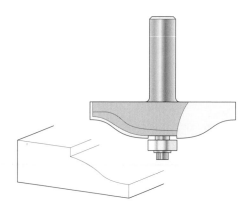

2–27. *Panel-raising is readily done with this cutter that shapes the panel field and reduces its thickness simultaneously. The surrounding frame is then assembled around the panel.*

Beading Cutters

These are common cutters used for producing a limited variety of decorative moldings for edges of chairs, shelves, frames, and tabletops (2–28). When they are matched up with reed cutters (which are used to cut semi-cylindrical molding), it is possible to join two parts together. By adjusting the height of subsequent passes, it is also possible to create repeat patterns for a decorative effect.

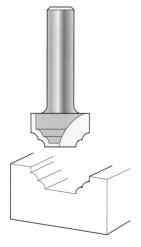

2–28. *A bead-ovolo cutter will produce a large range of decorative recesses and edge moldings of classic form.*

Decorative Cutters

Decorative cutters may be selected from an enormous range (2–29). When they are used either singly or by combining cutters of different shapes to create composite patterns, the possibilities are endless. Even repeated passes of the same cutter at different depths and widths may be used imaginatively to produce unique moldings, rails, or features associated with furniture.

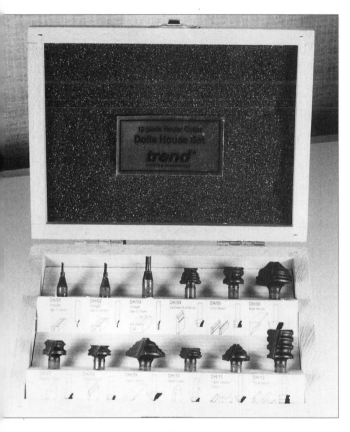

2–29. A boxed set of decorative cutters designed to produce an enormous variety of miniature moldings — especially for doll's house furniture.

Trimming Cutters

Most frequently, trimming cutters are found with end-fitted guide bearings, designed to trim surface laminates (2–30 to 2–32). One type, the pierce-and-trim cutter, has a dedicated purpose;

TRIMMING CUTTERS

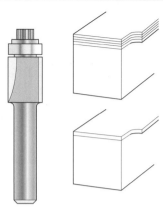

2–30. This bearing-guided cutter is ideal for trimming and cutting profiles, particularly for trimming plastics or plywood overlays.

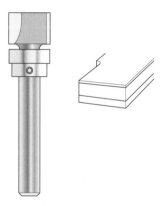

2–31. Running against a template, the bearing on this cutter will guide it as the cutter removes excess from the workpiece.

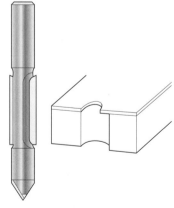

2–32. Piercing and trimming operations are combined in this cutter, with its base acting as a guide follower, similar to a bearing-guided cutter.

it is bearing-guided with an end-cutting feature. After an aperture is routed into a panel, say, of particleboard, the whole panel is covered with a plastic laminate. When the adhesive is completely dry, the pierce-and-trim cutter is plunged through the laminate and the bearing is drawn to the edge of the aperture. When the bearing makes contact with the edge, the cutter is traced around the aperture using its edge as a guide. The operation trims the laminate level with the aperture in the panel.

Rabbet (Rebate) Cutters

These cutters (refer to 2–21) are unbeatable for cutting rabbets (rebates) and recessing of many kinds, such as framing for pictures, windows, and cabinetwork. Pin-ended or ball-bearing guides are used predominantly in this form of cutter, the latter being the most useful, probably because of the built-in feature that allows bearing diameters to be changed. For a given width and diameter of cutter, the bearing end may be changed in order to vary the cutting depth. This is obviously a more economic system than using a collection of pin-ended cutters of various diameters.

Chamfering Cutters

Wherever a corner or edge needs to be relieved with a chamfer or a bevel, these cutters (2–33 and 2–34) save time and produce a good-looking profile. With stops fitted to limit the travel of the router, or the workpiece if you are using an inverted router in a table, it is possible to make a traditional "stopped" chamfer. Bevels may be predetermined by the form of the cutter profile at various angles, although the most common is at 45 degrees. Refer to Routerack Routing Sys-

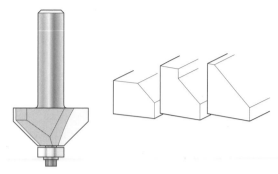

2–33. *For chamfering operations, a bearing-guided cutter is best, the size of the chamfer, or bevel, being controlled by the fence position or the router depth setting.*

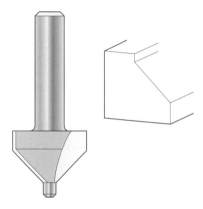

2–34. *A pin-ended cutter is useful for beveling the edges on plastic panels.*

tem on pages 119 to 121 for information on cutting chamfers using a router and specialized machines.

Coving Cutters

Coving cutters have a radiused bottom edge and are used for making channels with rounded bottoms, otherwise known as flutes (2–35). The cutter shape obviates the incorporation of a bearing, so generally coving cutters are used in fixed, inverted routers. Multiple progressive passes may be applied to make fluted columns found in fireplace surrounds and the like.

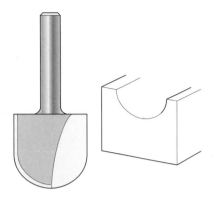

2–35. A typical coving cutter with a radiused cutting profile, available in many different sizes for decorative coved recessing.

Plug Cutters

When it is necessary to plug a counterbored hole containing a screw, a special cutter is used to produce a plug of the correct diameter to match the counterbore (2–36). A piece of scrap material of the same type as the workpiece is used to make the plug. If the workpiece is of natural wood, with care a plug can be cut from a similar material, even with matching grain to render the effect virtually undetectable.

2–36. Plug cutters are hollow in the center to create a plug for insertion into a matching hole. After the cutter is applied to the workpiece, the plug is detached by applying a sideways force with a screwdriver.

Plug cutters are designed exclusively for plunge-routing, being driven in perpendicular to the surface of the workpiece. It is then a simple matter to pry out the plug with a screwdriver and insert it into the counterbore. Any protruding part of the plug is trimmed away with a chisel.

Counterboring Cutters

A counterbore is a second hole bored after an initial drilling of a hole that accepts a screw or bolt. The first hole is a clearance diameter for the shank of the screw and the second is of a diameter big enough to accept the screw head. The holes should be concentric and, for this reason, this specially designed drill bit or cutter is made as a one-piece tool, drilling both the screw hole and counterbore simultaneously. The depth of the counterbore is then simply a matter of setting the plunge depth. Obviously one-piece cutters are more efficient (2–37); however, the fixed

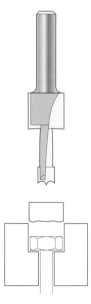

2–37. An example of counterboring to house a bolt head. After the bolt is fitted, it is possible to hide it by inserting a plug of appropriate diameter created by a plug cutter, as shown in 2–36.

diameters limit the size of screw compatibility and a busy carpenter may need to own a selection. Refer to Counterboring on page 98 for more information on this technique.

Jointing Cutters

Few systems of machine-jointing are superior to those available to the router. The production of two members with matching features to interlock or combine to make a joint is a facility that routers accomplish with accuracy and comparative ease. Of the several sets of jointing cutters available, two in particular offer high-quality results combined with practical application. One is the box-joint (otherwise known as a comb-joint) system. This is a set of five cutters about two inches in diameter fitted on an arbor with spacing collars separating the cutters (2–38). The

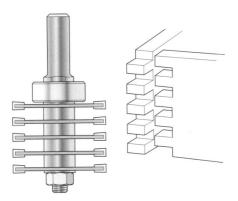

2–38. *Precision jointing for box corners is achieved with this box- (comb-) joint cutter. Its multiple tips set at widths to match the thickness of its cut allow both parts to be machined from the same cutter.*

cutters and collars guarantee the production of tongues and grooves of precisely the same width, allowing a perfect fit of two matching sides. These cutters are ideal for making boxes and trays comprised of materials up to two inches wide.

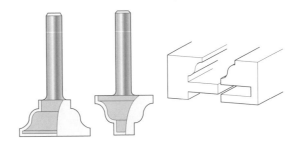

2–39. *Molding and scribing, otherwise known as "cope-and-stick" jointing, is possible with the set of cutters shown. The tenon-and-groove joint beneath the molding would be machined in a separate operation.*

Another notable set is the pair of framing cutters that perform the task of cutting a molding and scribing for the matching parts of a frame (2–39). (Because of the size of this cutter set and the nature of the operation, the best advice is to use it only with a fixed router.)

Grooving Cutters

Grooving cutters are used mostly for grooving but also for chamfering and engraving due to their V-shaped forms (2–40). Grooves of various widths may be cut by setting the cutter at different depths. Decorative effects are possible by machining grooves side by side along a panel or column. The cutter is not absolutely pointed because of a small flat ground at its end.

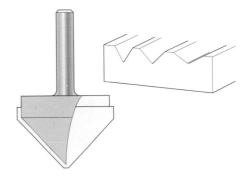

2–40. *Shaped to suit either chamfering or grooving, this cutter may be used to create decorative effects by multiple applications.*

Recessing Cutters

Where there is a need for shallow recesses, as in the case of fitting a hinge, the recess cutter, designed for end-and-face cutting in a plunge mode, is an efficient and practical tool (2–41). It is usual to combine this type of cutter used in this application with a template to ensure an accurately sized recess. After plunging to the required depth, the cutter's lateral-cutting facility allows the tracing of the outline of the recess by following the template.

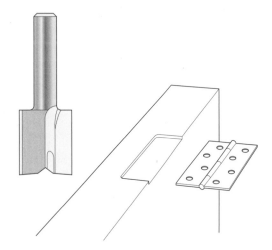

2–41. *Hinge-recessing is especially suitable for routing. A cutter with side- and end-cutting features is usually applied with a template to guide the router.*

Dovetail Cutters

Perhaps the most time-honored and highly respected woodworking joint is the dovetail, prized as a superb joint for drawer construction and other cabinetwork. Its physical strength and its appearance give pride to the maker, whether it is made by hand or machine. A certain amount of calculation and design are necessary depending on the size of the workpiece prior to the routing operation, as is the case with many other applications. Several manufacturers offer jigs specifically for the use of dove-

tail cutting, some requiring a specially designed cutter recommended for a particular system (2–42).

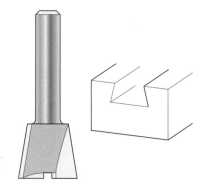

2–42. *Used for cutting sliding dovetails, this cutter will rout the groove for the shelves and shape the shelf ends.*

Cutters for Metals and Plastics

Routing metals may be accomplished with the appropriate cutters, as, for example, those used for trimming welds or deburring cutters. They may also be applied to fiberglass (glass-reinforced polyester) for shaping and trimming (2–43). Wood carvers find them useful for fine detail work.

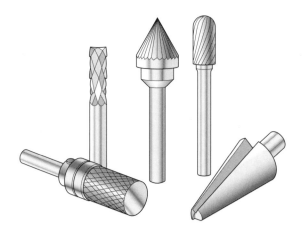

2–43. *A group of solid tungsten-carbide cutters designed for milling and shaping of metals and fiberglass (glass reinforced plastics). Refer to Chapter 4 for more information on cutting these materials.*

Inlaying Cutters

An especially interesting type of cutter comes as a set of bearings to add singly to the end of an inlay cutter (2–44). This makes available different depths of recess for inlaying stringing or lines. Various widths of recess may be produced on different positions on the workpiece by changing the plunge depth.

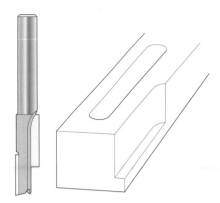

2–45. A mortise cutter may be used for deep recessing or mortising. As shown, the cutting edges are diametrically opposed and arranged at different heights.

Rosette (Roundel) Shapers

Rosettes, or roundels, are floral designs in wood used as decorative elements. They are produced from one plunged operation with a cutter made to suit the profile of the required pattern (2–46). Sets of cutters come in pairs and are attached by screws to the cutter body. Recommended speeds for this cutter—bearing in mind it may be up to four inches in diameter—are no more than 2,000 rpm in hardwood. Bear in mind that this means the peripheral speed is over 2,000 feet per minute!

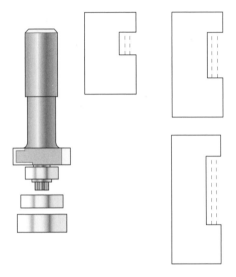

2–44. Variations in the depth and height of a recess are available with the inlaying assembly shown here. Bearings of different diameters are part of the set.

Mortise Cutters

Mortises for jointing with tenons or for creating recesses for door locks are produced with a cutter with staggered blades (2–45). The cutting edges are diametrically opposed and also arranged at different heights on the shaft. This helps relieve the strain on the shaft when deep cuts are made.

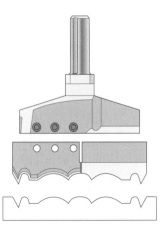

2–46. Three "flats" on the shank of a rosette shaper provide an area for the location of clamps with T-nuts.

Template Profilers

The bearing guide mounted on the shank above the template profiler is meant to run against a template. The oversized workpiece will be cut to the exact size of the template to which it has been attached.

Reversible-Tip Cutters

These are practical and economical cutters that double the life of a cutting edge by being sharpened on opposite edges (2–47). The tip is attached to the cutter body by screws and is both reversible, allowing the use of a second edge when the first has become dulled, and replaceable when both edges are blunt.

2–47. Reversible-tip cutters do just as their name suggests: When the cutting edge is blunted or damaged, the tip is unlocked by removal of the retaining screws and replaced in the reverse position.

Ovolo Cutters

The same-radius cutter is used for the production of ovolos (rounded convex moldings) and the rounding-over of panels and edge molding. (Refer to 2–19.) With or without a bearing guide, it is a very popular type of cutter, available with many variations on the simple theme of radius profiling.

Slot Cutters

Slot cutters are frequently fitted on arbors and may be combined with spacers for multiple grooving applications (2–48). Bearing guides are often used to obviate the need for a fence, and this makes it possible to apply smaller sizes in freehand mode. A range of diameters from which to choose is available from most suppliers. Extra care is advised when assembling the cutters on arbors to ensure that the cutter is arranged to cut in accordance with the direction of the rotating spindle.

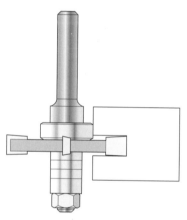

2–48. A slotter/groover assembled on an arbor with spacers arranged for a specific thickness of cutter. Wider cutters require fewer spacers, and different diameters of bearing will produce different depths of groove.

Arbor Combinations

An arbor is a special spindle made to accept one or more cutters that may be interchanged or combined with cutters of different diameters—with or without bearing guides and spacing collars—to create composite cutter arrangements. It is possible to build a collection of cutters, spacers, and bearings to customize a wide variety of applications, including slitting, trimming, tongue-and-grooving, and scribing (2–49 and 2–50).

2–49. Arbor combinations offer a less expensive range of cutters, because only one shaft, or arbor, is required for several cutter types. Also, the possibility of combining two or more cutters simultaneously can reduce machining time. Bearings, washers, and spacers may be intermixed with cutters to create a wide range of forms.

2–50. Another example of an arbor combination, showing slitting cutters in three thicknesses attached to the shaft with a bearing guide.

Care of Cutters

STORAGE

Cutters are valuable items that are easily damaged if mishandled. Cutters should never be allowed to jostle each other in a portable toolbox, for example. The cutting edges are vulner-able, particularly if brought into contact with other cutters, being equally hard. It is best to keep the cutters in the original packing if it is sturdy enough to protect those edges from accidental damage (2–51). If the cutter collection is likely to be static, kept in a cupboard in the workshop, for instance, then a simple board with holes drilled at intervals, in which to insert the shanks, is fine to store the cutters separately until they are needed. When acquired in sets, the cutters are often as not housed in strong boxes that separate them securely (2–52). Various designs of storage boxes are available from several sources with a range of sizes to suit the many shapes of cutter on offer (2–53). Any covers or lids should be lined with foam or similar material to further protect the cutting edge in case the cutter becomes dislodged from its housing (2–54).

As with any other steel tool, cutters are subject to rust, so after use and cleaning, they should be wiped or sprayed with a light oil to prevent oxi-

STORING CUTTERS

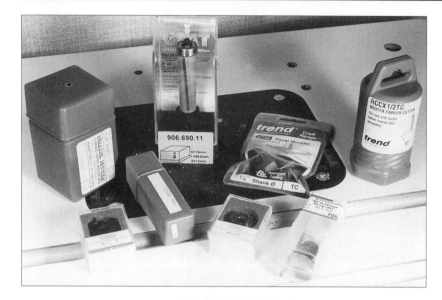

2–51. Most cutters come in strong plastic packs that might serve as permanent protective storage.

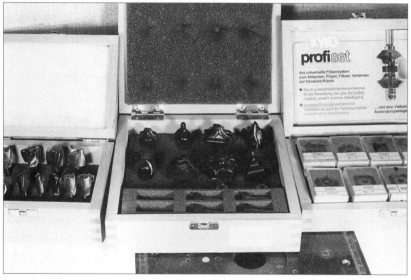

2–52. When bought in sets, cutters are as often as not supplied in wooden storage boxes. If this box is to be used for permanent storage, make sure that a silicon crystal bag or some other rust deterrent is added to protect the cutters from corrosion.

2–53. Plastic trays designed to hold a variety of cutters make excellent storage. Inserts are provided to suit various shank diameters. A light coating of oil and a dry drawer are essential as complements to this form of storage if corrosion is to be kept at bay.

(continued on following page)

STORING CUTTERS (CONTINUED)

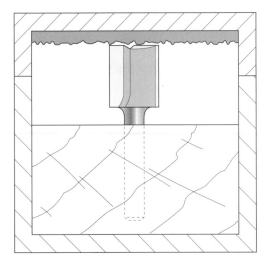

2–54. *Cross-section view of a storage box showing a cutter shank fitted into the base with a foam insert lining the lid to prevent damage to the tips.*

dization. Before using them again from storage, the protective oil should be wiped away to avoid staining the work.

MAINTENANCE

Cutting edges should be kept sharp at all times in order to operate efficiently. Apart from reducing strain on the collet, lessening wear on the bearings, and being easier to feed into the work, a keenly sharp edge has the advantage of leaving a satisfactory surface finish on the workpiece (2–55).

Fortunately, modern hones make it possible to sharpen by hand even the hard TCT blades, the techniques for which are detailed on pages 62 to 64.

Some causes of wear are reducible, even if not entirely avoidable, by the following means.

Heat, if generated excessively during routing operations, will quickly degrade the sharpness of the cutter. Overheating will usually occur if too slow a feed rate is applied, allowing the compacting of waste and thus increasing friction

between the cutter body and the work surface. So check the feed rate by the feel of resistance to the cutter and also by listening to the sound produced by the action. (Refer to Routing Speeds and Feeds on pages 95 and 96 for more information on feed rate.)

Still on the subject of reducing overheating, any resinous deposits or waste chips that might

2–55. *A simple way to test the sharpness of the cutter. The test piece is soft cedar—not the easiest of woods to cut this way.*

have become jammed into the corners of the cutter flutes should be removed (2–56). A sharp knife will help in this case, provided it is used delicately and with caution. Several proprietary brands of cutter cleaners are available to free gummy residues and the like from the cutter surfaces. Spray-on solvents are very effective for the removal of resin deposits.

A bearing-guided cutter, that is, one with a pilot fitted below or above the cutter, on the shank, needs special mention (2–57). Maintenance is minimal and probably obvious. The pilot should be kept clean and freely rotating in order for it to perform as a smooth guiding contact in template tracing projects. If trimming

2–56. *Cleaning away resinous deposits that have become impacted in the corners of the cutter. A sharp blade is used for this, with caution.*

laminates, allow glues used for the lamination to dry completely before commencing the routing operation; this will help to ensure clean contact with the bearing. If adhesives, resins, dust, etc. do become attached to the bearing, it is best to try to remove them as delicately as possible. No attempt should be made to soak away the deposits by immersing them in a solvent cleaner, as this would release essential lubricants from the bearing. Better to scrape away the residues with a carefully applied sharp knife (2–58). It should be remembered that the bearing is an expendable item and, if there is any doubt about its efficiency, it should be replaced. Failure of the bearing to revolve freely will seriously jeopardize its effectiveness as a guide.

SHARPENING CUTTERS

Any blemish on the sharp edge of a cutter will be detrimental to its performance, in terms of productive cutting and finish of the workpiece. Damage of this kind, however it is caused, is usually found as chips and abrasions on the extreme cutting edge. Examination with a magnifying lens may reveal some alarming defects after just a few passes (2–59). Fortunately, providing that the faults are not major, it is possible to resharpen the cutter by honing the tips with an abrasive stone. The word "stone" is something of a misnomer today because we rarely use a natural stone for sharpening. In fact, most stones (also referred to as hones) are man-made even if they are composed of natural materials. Good examples currently available are ceramic and diamond-coated stones, either of which may be used successfully to reconstitute a damaged cutting edge (2–60).

Both ceramic and diamond-coated stones are best lubricated with water to help the honing operation and float away the debris produced by

REMOVING RESIN FROM BEARING-GUIDED CUTTERS

2–57. Cutters with bearings. Above, a cutter with an end-fitted bearing; below, one with a shank-fitted bearing. Both do the same job; that is, the bearing runs against a template or prepared edge, acting as a guide to cut an outline or peripheral shape.

2–58 (right). Small deposits of resin and other debris can become embedded in the nooks and crannies of bearing cases; they should be removed with careful application of a sharp knife.

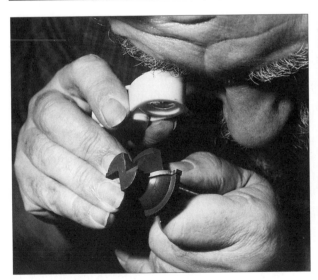

2–59. Inspection of the cutting edge is best carried out with a magnifying lens.

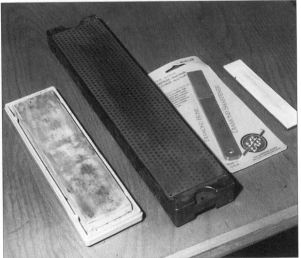

2–60. Hones suitable for sharpening router cutters. From left to right: a bench-top ceramic stone, a bench-top diamond hone, a hand-applied diamond stone, and a hand-applied ceramic slip.

the rubbing action of the cutter against the stone (2–61).

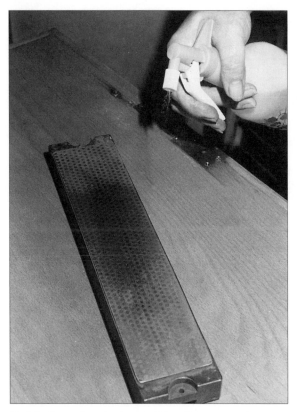

2–61. *Preparing the hone with a fine spray of water. This lubricates the surface and washes away the waste particles generated during the sharpening process.*

Some cautionary wisdom should be borne in mind before embarking on the honing process. Only the face of the cutter should be treated with the hand-honing process, and it should never be taken to a bench-grinding wheel to sharpen. A bench grinder is much too aggressive to impart a small correction to a tip with sufficient control to be effective. Any loss of symmetry in the cutter, all too easily achieved by grinding the tips unequally, would result in imbalance, leading to almost certain disaster. For the same reasons, the sides or ends of the cutter tip should not be treated by grindstone or by hand-honing.

When honing the flat face of the cutter, place it on the water-lubricated hone and proceed to slide the cutter slowly along the length of the abrasive plate while keeping firm and constant downward pressure (2–62 to 2–64). After several passes, inspect the cutter; it should be apparent by the fresh, shiny areas where contact with the hone was made (2–65). By inspecting the effect of this abrasive action, any necessary adjustments should be made to the location of the cutter face on the hone or downward pressure should be applied to ensure that eventually the whole face will become clean with complete restoration to the damaged edge. Of course, in keeping with the foregoing comments about symmetrical edges, it is important to impart the same treatment to the opposite cutter tip, even if it is not as damaged as the first. This is in order to maintain balance and equality.

If the cutter has a bearing guide attached, it must be removed before the operator attempts to sharpen the edges.

Installing Cutters

As a rule, when fitting cutters, a strict sequence should be followed with regard to the collet and cutter assembly. When using a multi-slit type of collet, it is essential to fit the collet and the compression nut together before inserting them as a unit into the spindle (2–66 and 2–67). If this procedure is not followed and the collet is fitted into the spindle first, there is the possibility of misaligning the nut, collet, and spindle. If the nut is applied cross-threaded on the spindle, for instance, there will be inevitable distortion of some component in the assembly—probably the collet.

A word about the cutter prior to installation: If the cutter is new, there may well be a protective shield of soft plastic enclosing it. Removal of this protection should be done by slitting the plastic

2–62. *Inspection before the honing process. The face is not clean and the edge is imperfect.*

2–63. *Commencing the honing stroke. As much as possible of the "flat" of the cutting face is in contact with the surface of the hone.*

2–64. *The end of the first stroke with the cutter now at the opposite end of the hone. Try to keep firm contact between the faces of the cutter and the hone throughout the movement. Draw the cutter back to the starting point and repeat the operation until the cutting edge is sharp and clean and without blemish.*

2–65. *After a series of strokes on the hone, the cutting face is clean and shining with a much-improved cutting edge.*

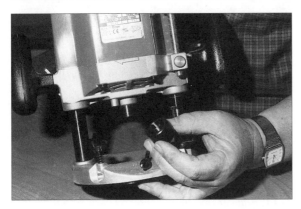

2–66. *In the case of the collet/compression nut combination, it is best to assemble the nut and collet before insertion into the spindle to ensure correct alignment of the three parts.*

2–67. *Free-running threads ease installation and help to ensure the correct alignment of collet and spindle before the cutter is fitted.*

between the flutes rather than risk damaging the cutting edge (2–68 and 2–69). If cut in such a way as to pry it away in one piece, the shield can be replaced to give continued protection while in storage.

Before the cutter is installed, several things

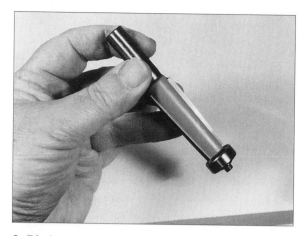

2–70. *A checklist for inspection should include cutting edges, bearing guides, shank, and the cutter's general cleanliness.*

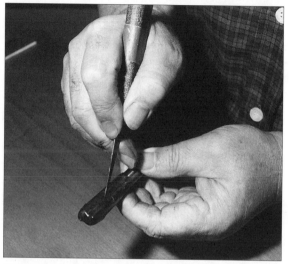

2–68. *With discretion, a sharp knife may be used to slit the waxy, protective sleeve coating a new cutter.*

following: the cutting edge for imperfections; overall cleanliness; that the bearing guides are free-running; and that the shank does not have any faults. Also check the collet for any blemish inside or out, rejecting it if damage is detected, and to ensure that the size of its internal diameter matches the cutter. Check the compression nut for compatibility with the collet and spindle (2–71) and for clean threads and undamaged flats, to ensure a non-slip application of the

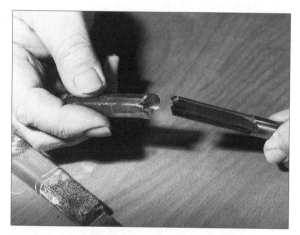

2–69. *Providing the knife is applied with some forethought, it is possible to replace the waxy coating to act as a protective sleeve for future use.*

should be checked (2–70). (Don't forget to wear a glove for this; remember, the cutting edge should be sharp enough to cut flesh.) Check the

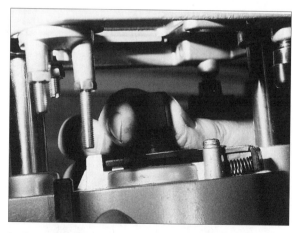

2–71. *A finger and thumb test to check free running of the nut/spindle assembly. Prior to this, the nut should be inspected to see that the flats are not damaged, ensuring secure application of the wrench.*

wrench (also known as a spanner). If the inspection reveals no flaws in these components, the installation may proceed.

Begin by inverting the router by standing it on its top, if possible (refer to 2–13). If not, then lay it on its side oriented to leave clear access to the collet assembly (2–72 and 2–73). Presuming that the collet has been installed correctly, the shank of the cutter may be inserted into it (2–74). All that is of concern at this stage is to

INSTALLING CUTTERS

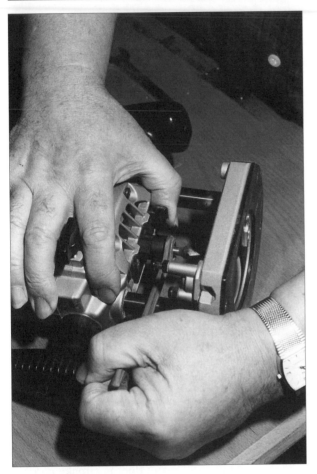

2–72. A sliding lock is applied with the thumb to lock the spindle, while the wrench is used to tighten or loosen the compression nut.

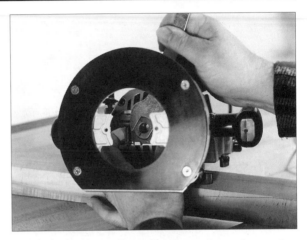

2–73. In this case, the finger of the left hand is used to slide the spindle clamp into locking position as the wrench is applied to the collet. No compression nut is used in this particular system.

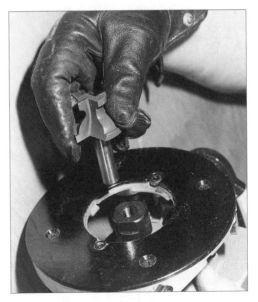

2–74. If handled clumsily, a sharp cutter is likely to cause injury to fingers. Gloves are a wise precaution for the job of cutter installation.

(continued on following page)

CORRECT   INCORRECT

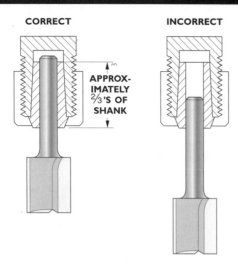

APPROX-
IMATELY
⅔'S OF
SHANK

2–75. *As the illustration shows, it is desirable for at least two-thirds of the cutter shank to be inserted into the spindle for security and to avoid damage to the collet.*

2–76. *Distortion of the collet is possible if the cutter is not inserted correctly, as shown here.*

2–77. *Tightening the compression nut. Both wrenches are being applied here. The left one is used for the compression nut, and the right one to hold the spindle. It is possible to bring both wrenches to the same side of the spindle to operate them simultaneously with one hand, leaving the other hand free to insert or remove the cutter.*

decide how far into the collet the shank is to be inserted. With some qualification, the general rule is: as much as possible. If a shank can be inserted as far as the shoulders of the cutter, then it should be withdrawn slightly, to clear the fluting from the collet jaws. (Adjusting the cutter away from the collet jaws also helps to avoid the jamming of waste against, possibly directly, into the collet during the routing operation.

Some cutters are designed with a small radius joining the body of the cutter to its shank. If the cutter is thrust up close to the collet, it is possi-

ble that this radius may ruin the collet jaws when they are compressed. It is also preferable to ensure that the end of the shank does not make contact with the bottom of the spindle recess, as undesirable vibration may be transmitted through the cutter. Withdrawal of about ¹⁄₁₆ inch is therefore recommended in this case also. Aim for not less than two-thirds of the cutter shank to be held in the collet and, as was stressed earlier, the more the better (2–75).

Sometimes, a routing setup may give a smaller cutter insufficient projection through the sub-base or table to achieve the required depth. Never be tempted to achieve the desired extra depth by withdrawing the cutter to compensate for the discrepancy. This could lead to a whole catalog of problems. With inadequate grip by the collet, the cutter could become detached, with obvious dire results. Compressing the collet with incomplete contact along its length could cause its deformation (2–76).

Similar caution should be exercised when tightening the compression nut to grip the shank of the cutter. It is normal to tighten the nut with a wrench provided for that purpose, with which it is possible to exert more than necessary force to hold the cutter securely (2–77). Speaking of the wrench, make sure it is the correct size to fit the compression nut, preferably the nut supplied with the router. It is unusual for the average workshop to have equipment to measure the amount of force being applied, so, as is so often the case, common sense is applied. If the wrench is hurting the hand that is applying the force, then it could be hurting the shank by driving the collet into it. When first applying the cutter to the workpiece, be sensitive to the possibility of the cutter slipping instead of rotating and cutting correctly, as this would be the first sign of insufficient pressure of the collet. Rotation of the spindle without corresponding movement of the cutter is certain to mean damage to one or all of the parts in the assembly if the cutter is being prevented from rotating.

Yes, it has been said elsewhere, but here it comes again with no apology for repetition: Do not try to assemble or use incompatible collets and cutters; it makes sense to mark them in some obvious way (2–78) and to keep the different sizes separated permanently.

SHAFT LOCKS

Depending on the make and model of the router, different shaft locks are operated in different ways.

There are some that need two wrenches: one to hold the shaft while the other operates the compression nut. More recently a system has become available, arguably superior, that uses a sliding lock to prevent the spindle from turning during the operation of the compression nut (2–79). The sliding-lock mechanism is spring-loaded to return the

2–78. *If collets and cutters of metric and imperial diameters are likely to get mixed, it is wise to mark them in some way in order to ensure correct identification. A dab of paint on the end of the shank should suffice.*

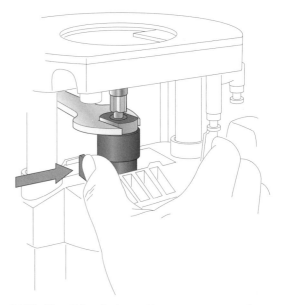

2–79. *The sliding lock on this router prevents the spindle from turning while the compression nut is being tightened.*

lock to its neutral position after use, making a very efficient and rapid operation.

Removing Cutters from Collets

When it comes to the removal of the cutter, it is simply a matter of reversing the installation procedure, unless there is a problem of a sticking cutter. If the cutter is unwilling to be withdrawn, some encouragement may be necessary. Gentle tapping on the spindle, the compression nut, and the cutter itself should help. Use a piece of wood in the same manner as a chisel and strike it with a hammer (2–80). If this does not free the cutter, take a wrench—large enough to span the shank but smaller than the cutter body—and try leverage. Using something such as a piece of cardboard or plastic as a cushion (2–81 and 2–82), avoid contact between the cutter edges and the wrench. This should be enough to coax the cutter out of the collet. Inspect the shank of the cutter for some flaw that might cause the collet to jam and examine the collet for the same reason. Better to discard either, or both, as dictated by the damage, if the problem persists.

2–80. One method of removing a stubborn cutter is to strike it with a blow from a mallet using a wooden "chisel." A hardwood stick is suitable, being tough enough but not hard enough to damage the cutter.

2–81. Another method of cutter removal is to use a wrench as a lever. It should be large enough to span the cutter shank but smaller than the cutter diameter. A cushion made from fiberboard or something similar is essential to prevent damage to the cutter.

2–82. Here the cushioned wrench is positioned around the shank and under the cutter head to apply leverage.

CHAPTER 3

Workpiece Clamping Techniques

Factors That Determine Clamping Technique

The workpiece has to be secured to the surface when the router is applied freehand. This can be done with various types of commercial and user-made clamps and techniques, depending on these factors: the type of material being routed, the size of the workpiece, and the nature of the operation. Each is discussed below.

MATERIAL

If the router is being used on wood, it is possible that clamping must be firm but gentle so as not to bruise the fibers by depressing with the clamp. Some additional pads placed between the clamping jaw and the work surface to act as cushions are then advisable (3–1). With man-made boards, there is less need to add protection of this kind and the clamp may be applied without extra cushioning.

WORKPIECE SIZE

Where large workpieces are concerned, clamps may need to extend over a large surface or be attached to a jig, bench, or work base. Small

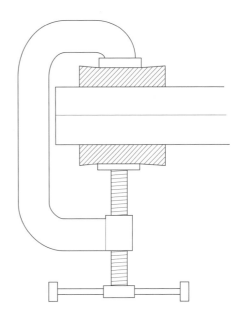

3–1. Pads are placed next to the clamping jaws to prevent bruising of the workpiece surface.

workpieces, on the other hand, may well need special jigs or clamps devised exclusively for that operation (3–2).

OPERATION

Various types of clamps can be used in different ways, depending on the nature of the operation. Remember, however, that for surface routing, clamping arrangements need to be below the top

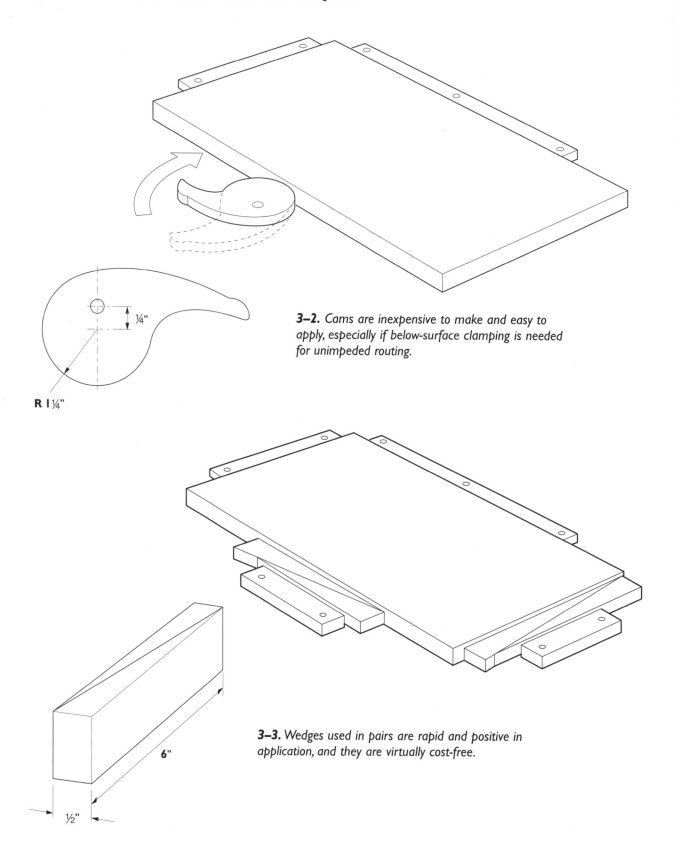

R 1¼"

¼"

3–2. *Cams are inexpensive to make and easy to apply, especially if below-surface clamping is needed for unimpeded routing.*

3–3. *Wedges used in pairs are rapid and positive in application, and they are virtually cost-free.*

6"

½"

of the workpiece in order to avoid contact with the cutter (3–3).

If a repetitious operation is planned on many workpieces of a similar shape and size, the likeli-hood is that a template will be involved, in addition to clamping jigs that are dedicated to that job (3–4).

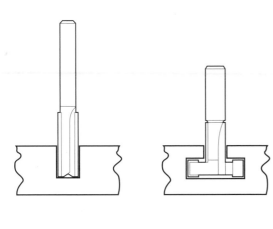

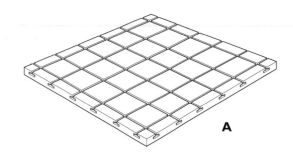

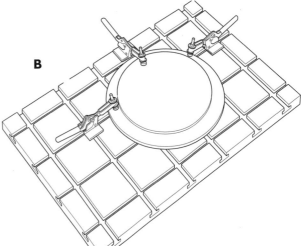

3–4. *Routing a workpiece using different clamping applications. (A) A grooved work board with a grid, or network, of grooves to facilitate multi-positioning of T-nut clamps. The workpiece will be attached to the work board. (B) Three toggle clamps arranged on a grooved work board to effect clamping of a circular workpiece. (C) Speed clamping using one clamp arranged to press the workpiece sideways into a similarly shaped pattern. (D) The toggle clamp, T-nut, bolts, and spacers, as shown in applications b and c.*

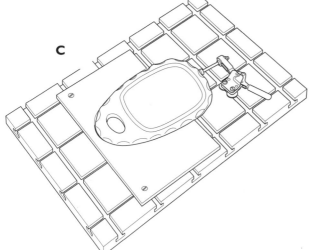

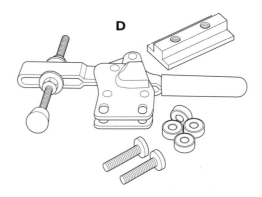

Types of Clamp

C-CLAMPS

So-called because of their resemblance to the letter C, C-clamps* have been the woodworker's friend for centuries and they have as much, if not more, use today, as the router user's companion (3–5).

QUICK-ACTION CLAMPS

Quick-action clamps (3–6) are applicable in the same way and in similar setups as their older C-clamp cousins. They are more appealing than the C-clamp, because they generally occupy less space, have greater maneuverability and, as their name implies, are faster to apply. Several types are available (3–7).

C-, QUICK-ACTION, AND TOGGLE CLAMPS

3–5. Various sized collection of C-clamps, which are cast-steel frames with square threaded shafts.

3–6. A one-handed application with a "squeeze"-action clamp featuring large padded clamping faces.

*In the United States, these clamps are referred to as C-clamps because of their resemblance to the letter C. In Europe, they are referred to as G-clamps because they are obviously also similar in shape to the letter G.

(continued on following page)

TOGGLE CLAMPS

Toggle clamps are available in a wide variety of designs employing the principles of mechanical movement involving pivots, levers, and over-center clamping actions (3–8). They are available with their mounting plates set at different angles to the clamp body and with movement transferred from the lever to the buffer through an ingenious arrangement of toggles. The fixing of the operating position of these clamps allows for rapid use in repetitive routing applications.

Some toggle clamps come with mounting plates shaped like an inverted "T," permitting their insertion into a work board with an appropriate network of slots. (Refer to 3–4c and d.) This makes for rapid reorientation of the clamping points. Making a slotted work board is a straightforward affair involving the use of only two cutters and a straight guide. (Refer to 3–4 a and b.)

C-, QUICK-ACTION, AND TOGGLE CLAMPS (CONTINUED)

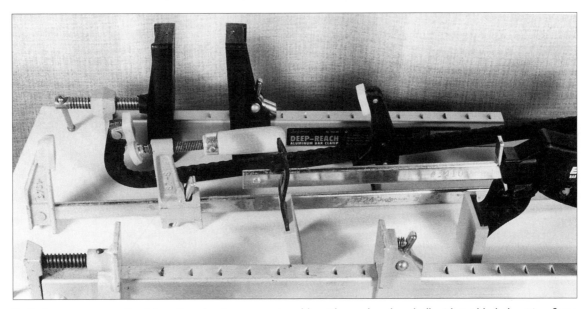

3–7. An assortment of quick-action clamps, some operable with one hand and all with padded clamping faces.

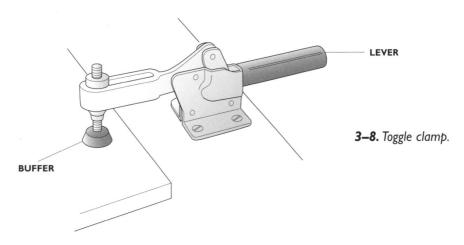

LEVER

BUFFER

3–8. Toggle clamp.

WEDGES AND CAM CLAMPS

If the surface of the workpiece is to be routed, any clamping system that protruded above the work surface would obstruct the movement of the router. At least two uncomplicated clamps exist for just this type of work, both user-made. They are wedge and cam clamps, and both are as old as the hills! (Refer to 3–2 and 3–3.)

Another advantage of user-made clamps—assuming that they are made from wood—is that accidental contact with a cutter will only damage the wedge, an easily replaced item.

SOCKET CLAMPS

A more sophisticated clamp that achieves the same function of securing the workpiece without protruding above the surface but by a very different means is the socket clamp (3–9). Here, instead of the usual pressure pad, against which the buffer is pressed, there is a projecting plug of round section. This is intended for insertion into the edge of a workpiece or work board and then clamped in the usual way, with the screw-operated buffer drawn up against the underside of a bench or work top.

HOLD-DOWNS

Hold-downs (3–10) are another form of clamp used on workpieces during routing applications.

BENCH DOGS

Another ancient clamping principle with wide applications is the bench-dog system (3–11). So-called "dogs" are stops that are inserted in holes bored into bench tops. They may be round, square, or rectangular and are retained at the chosen height above the bench top by a spring-loaded device. Holes to match the dog are bored at intervals in rows along the bench top in line with similar dogs inserted into the end vise. Many irregular shapes may also be accommodated, including the temporary securing of small router tables if they are fitted on a mounting board.

With a clamping range as wide as the bench is long and with potential for below-surface clamping, it is hardly surprising that the system is still popular.

SOCKET CLAMPS, HOLD-DOWNS, AND BENCH DOGS

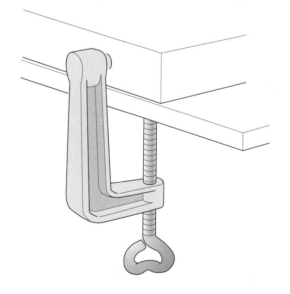

3–9. Socket clamp.

(continued on following page)

SOCKET CLAMPS, HOLD-DOWNS, AND BENCH DOGS (CONTINUED)

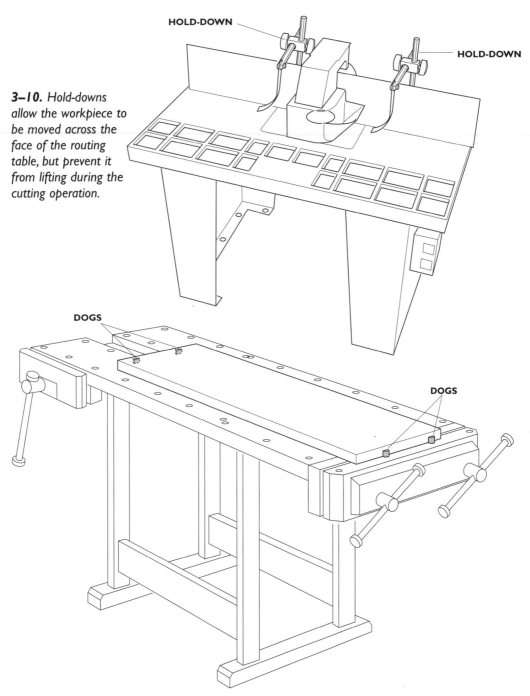

3–10. *Hold-downs allow the workpiece to be moved across the face of the routing table, but prevent it from lifting during the cutting operation.*

3–11. *Bench-top clamping applications are available with "dogs," as shown here. The dogs are placed in prelocated holes in the bench, with two clamping ones positioned in the movable vise jaw.*

WORKBENCH BOARD CLAMPING TECHNIQUES

If a workpiece's edges are to be routed to form decorative or functional molding, such as shelving or rabbets on door frames, the workpiece may be too big to handle on a conventional routing table. If it is necessary to take the router to the work, it is also desirable that the workpiece be held in an upright position, presenting its edge upwards. This permits the machining to be performed with the router presented in the vertical position with normal two-handed control.

To effect this practical method, all that is required is the drilling of the workbench leg at the opposite end of the bench from the side vise (3–12). Holes are produced at regular intervals on a vertical line in the center of the leg, into which is placed a peg to support the free end of the workpiece. It is an easy matter to secure the workpiece horizontally in the vise while supporting the other end at an appropriately selected peg height.

VACUUM CLAMPING

Not as modern as may be thought, vacuum clamping offers many advantages over pressure clamps and vises (3–13). As long as the workpiece (or the work board to which it is attached) is flat and smooth, holding it down by vacuum pressure can be very efficient. Vacuum extraction can be provided by an ordinary vacuum cleaner fitted with suitable connections; alternatively, systems for specific purposes are available, ranging widely in cost, size, and application.

Whichever type of extractor is used, unless it is purchased as a complete kit it is necessary for the user to make his or her own "chuck." The basic vacuum chuck is a plate or tablet with its surface

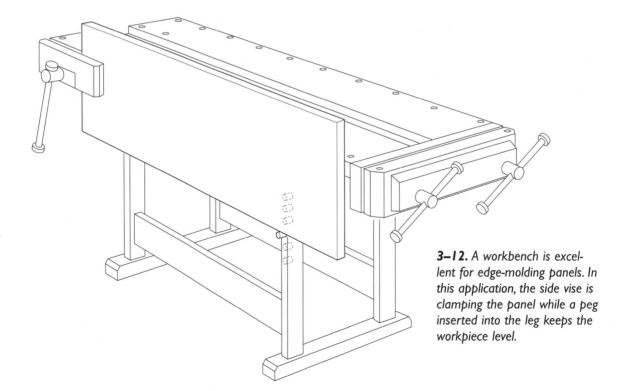

3–12. A workbench is excellent for edge-molding panels. In this application, the side vise is clamping the panel while a peg inserted into the leg keeps the workpiece level.

laid out with a cell (a small bounded space or cavity) or divided into multiple cells, each periphery of which is enclosed by a pressure-sensitive sealing strip. A rubber-type material such as neoprene is ideal for gasket production. Lengths of round-section molding may be housed in channels cut to a shallow depth, allowing the seal to protrude slightly to meet the underside of the workpiece in order to create the closed cell (refer to 3–13b and c). A flat strip with self-adhesive backing may be used as an alternative to the round-section type. This type of molding requires only surface contact, is quicker to make, and is efficient, providing that the chuck table has a clean, smooth surface. Through a port placed somewhere within the vacuum cell, underneath the workpiece, air is withdrawn by the vacuum extractor and operates the clamping action.

In general, freehand routing applied to a flat surface requires constant downward pressure and horizontal movement, and this is ideally suited

VACUUM-CLAMPING TECHNIQUES

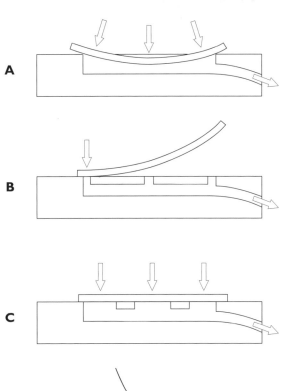

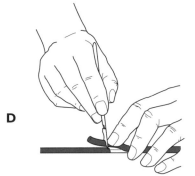

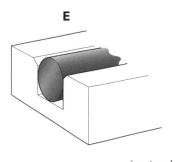

3–13. A vacuum-clamping operation requires the observation of several principles. Shown here are three applications. *(A)* has insufficient support in the center of the clamp, allowing the workpiece to sag. *(B)* has insufficient surface area affected by the vacuum. *(C)* is best, giving adequate support for the workpiece combined with sufficient orifices for the withdrawal of air to create the vacuum. *(D)* and *(E)* show the insertion of neoprene or other rubber-based gasket material into grooves to provide sealed cells for vacuum clamping.

(continued on following page)

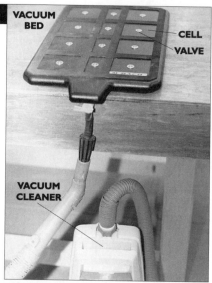

3–15. Fast-action clamping is the virtue of a vacuum bed. Add to this the facility to operate the system with an ordinary vacuum cleaner and its appeal is obvious.

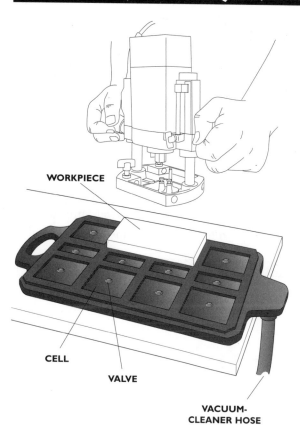

3–14. Vacuum clamping using a specially made device operating by the attachment of a standard vacuum cleaner. When a cell is covered by a flat workpiece, contact opens the valve in the center of each cell and vacuum pressure is activated.

3–16. Prior to applying a routing operation, the workpiece is smoothed, leveled, and cleaned with an orbital sander.

to vacuum-clamping methods (3–14). Even modest vacuum cleaners can exert enough suction to prevent lateral movement of the workpiece during surface routing, but care must be taken not to lift it, since the seal is broken very easily in this type of setup.

MINI-MACH VACUUM CLAMP

A quick-acting and portable vacuum clamp, the Mini-Mach (3–15) operates efficiently connected to a modest domestic vacuum cleaner. The vacuum bed is divided into cells, each of which contains a valve that remains closed until it is opened by downward pressure from the workpiece. With a capacity to hold flat workpieces from about 4-foot square down to less than 4-inch square, the Mini-Mach is obviously an asset to any routing workshop. All that is necessary to operate it is to switch on the power to the vacuum cleaner and place the flat workpiece over the cells in the clamping bed. The vacuum clamping force is effective within each cell that the workpiece covers, allowing work to be carried out on the surface of the secured workpiece (3–16).

4

Wood, Metal, and Plastic Cutting Guidelines

The following information describes the cutting characteristics of the most commonly routed materials and the manner of their treatment in routing operations.

Solid Wood

Wood in its many classifications is probably the most popular material for both professional and amateur use, perhaps because of its qualities as a structurally sound, functional, and handsome material, with few associated problems as a machinable commodity (4–1).

Being a natural organic substance, it does impose limits on the designer and the machinist, who need to be aware of its density, dryness, and grain direction before embarking on a project in which wood plays a significant part.

Hardwoods, as may be expected, take a greater toll on the cutter's sharp edges and also impose lower speeds and cutter feeds if satisfactory results are to be obtained. Softwoods, often

4–1. Many and various woods, hard and soft, are all routable, although—as in all woodworking applications—the more suitable the material, the better it works and the better the finish. Straight-grained, knot-free wood is recommended.

TABLE 4–1.

Cutter Diameter (Inches)	Router speed (Revolutions Per Minute)
¹⁄₁₆ to ⁵⁄₁₆	16,000 to 24,000 rpm
³⁄₈ to 1 inch	4,000 to 22,000 rpm
over 1 inch	(larger routers only) 8,000 to 14,000 rpm

abrasive and fibrous with corresponding difficulties, are not always as easy as their designation suggests. Nevertheless, as a general rule they may be machined at a higher speed than harder woods. (Refer to Table 4–1 and Chapter 6 for more information on routing speeds.) If planning to use either dense or tough woods, it is best to acquire TCT (tungsten-carbide-tipped) cutters.

In keeping with any other machining operation, routing with the grain is easier than routing across it, although the router copes with the latter better than many woodworking power tools. This is due to the high speed attainable by the router and the comparatively small amounts of material removed by each revolution.

Cutter and Router Speed Guidelines

If a proper speed is not used when routing wood and man-made boards, conditions such as tearout and workpiece burning may occur. Refer to Table 4–1 to determine a suitable speed for cutting at moderate depths in softwood, hardwood, and man-made boards. Always exercise caution when making this determination; that is, use the lower speed, shallower depth of cut, and slower feed rate.

Man-Made Boards

In this category may be included: (1) medium density fiberboard (MDF), a material available in thicknesses from ½ to 1 inch that is used to make furniture and cabinetwork; (2) plywood, plies of wood glued together in a sandwich-like fashion that are used for general and furniture construction; (3) chipboard, made from compressed wood particles; and (4) hardboard, or Masonite, a material generally used for drawer bottoms, panel backing, and siding and cabinet parts (4–2).

The most commonly used man-made material, for many good reasons, is MDF. It is structurally sound, has no grain or knots, rarely shows any physical defects, has consistent density, is rigid, flat, and smooth, machines readily (generally receiving a fine finish from the cutter), and is relatively cheap. No wonder it is popular; can it be the perfect board?

Recently, there have been many criticisms against the use of MDF due to the alleged risks associated with the dust generated in cutting or abrading it. Health and safety regulations differ from country to country, but contrary to workshop gossip, I have discovered nothing on official record banning the use of MDF, providing it is machined or processed in controlled conditions.

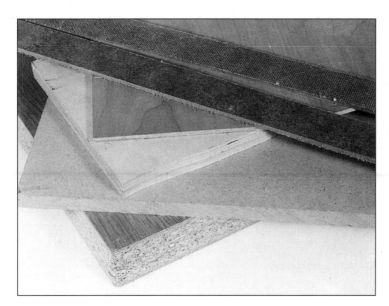

4–2. Most man-made materials of a wood-based type will machine well. Generally, tungsten-carbide cutters will perform best and more durably, because of the highly abrasive nature of particleboard and laminated surfaces.

Whether using natural wood or man-made materials, wise operators will protect themselves from dust from whatever source. Any air-borne dust is likely to be harmful, particularly if they are exposed to it for a considerable time. (For more information, refer to For Safety's Sake on pages 139 to 144.)

MDF allows great speeds in terms of cutting and feeding, with a predictably good finish. Although MDF has nothing in the way of eye appeal, and therefore is less usable in exposed situations without further extensive surface treatment, it is excellent for template use. The edge left from a routing cutter on MDF is usually clean enough to act as a guide for a bearing with no further treatment.

When routing plywood, consider the grain direction on the outside veneers as if it were solid wood in order to assess the effect of the cutting action.

Metals

As one might expect, metals are best machined with carbide cutters specially designed for the needs of the specific metal. Some special HSS (high-speed-steel) cutters have been developed for use with anodized aluminum, used frequently in window-frame manufacturing. The most appropriate cutters (more correctly called burrs, or rasps, for this application) are those made from solid carbide (4–3).

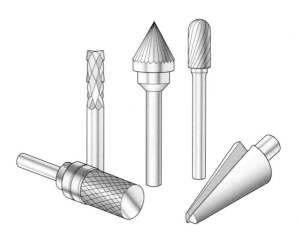

4–3. These solid tungsten-carbide cutters are designed for the milling and shaping of metals and fiberglass.

Plastics and Related Laminates

Polyvinyl chloride (PVC) is a material used especially for pipes and electrical insulation. Polyvinyl chloride (PVC) derivatives, as used in the widow-manufacturing industries, may be cut with special HSS single-flute helical cutters for plunge slotting and drilling (4–4). Single- or double- straight-fluted TCT (tungsten-carbide-tipped) cutters will also cut this material satisfactorily in surface milling applications.

Fiberglass (also referred to as glass fiber) can be shaped, cut, milled, drilled, and finished with cutters similar to those used on metal. They are usually made from solid carbide. (Refer to 4–3.)

4–4. A cutter with a single, helical flute used for deep entry into aluminum or PVC extrusions.

CHAPTER 5 Routing Applications

Freehand Routing

In freehand mode, the router is controlled by hand, with or without a template combined with a guide bush or ball-bearing guide. (For more information about the latter, refer to Templates on pages 109 to 114.) If a fixed-base router is being used, only one area of control is involved, that of steering the machine in the required direction. In the case of a plunge router, in addition to directional control (5–1 and 5–2), the cutting depth may be adjusted simultaneously by

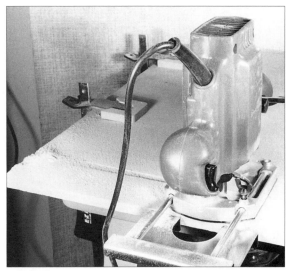

5–2. Halfway through the grooving process. Notice that without the connected dust extractor, the dust from the cutter heaps up behind the machine.

pressing down or releasing the motor housing in order to cause it to slide down or up on the plunge bars. This represents an easier method of cutter withdrawal than having to lift the fixed-base router off the surface. Adjusting the cutter depth on a fixed-based router may be accomplished by raising one side of its base while resting the opposite side on the workpiece (5–3).

Straight-line routing is readily achieved in freehand mode by attaching the side fence, an accessory that is normally supplied with the router (5–4 to 5–6).

SIDE FENCE

5–1. A plunge router used freehand with a side fence set at a prescribed distance from the edge of the workpiece in order to produce a parallel groove.

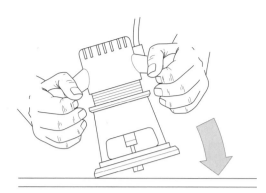

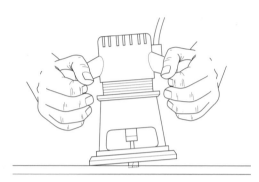

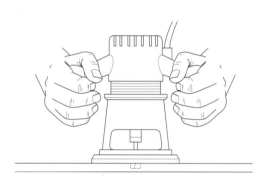

5–3. *With no plunge facility on a fixed-base router, cutting depth may be applied by rocking the base to produce a plunge effect, as shown.*

It is advisable to limit the application of freehand routing to the smaller-sized machines—routers less than 1¾ horsepower. Freehand routing requires a degree of muscular effort combined with coordination of hand and eye. As an exercise to develop confidence—and that indescribable asset "feel"—freehand routing has great benefits.

Generally, the freehand router is applied in vertical mode, that is, with the base placed on a level workpiece of some sort. Both hands are

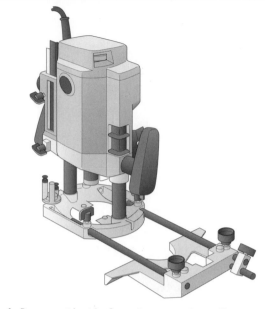

5–4. *Router with side fence incorporating a fine-adjustment control.*

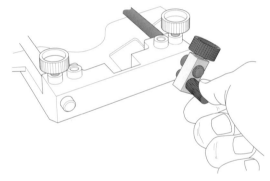

5–5. *The fine adjuster enables precise control to be made.*

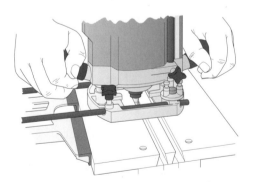

5–6. *Cutting a pin in the end of a shelf to suit a groove in a sliding dovetail joint using a side fence setup on a router.*

used for maximum control, unless the router has a D-shaped handle. (Refer to Handles, Locks, and Switches on pages 23 to 27 for more information on D-shaped handles.) In this application, there is a choice of following by eye a marked or imagined line with an appropriate cutter to create some recess, reed, or coving. The side fence, mentioned above, works admirably in this respect. Unrestricted movement in manual operation allows some flexibility to the user, offering possibilities for creative work.

Fixed-Router Techniques

INVERTED ROUTING

The term "inverted routing" simply means that the base of the router is uppermost, and this invariably means it will be attached to some device in order to maintain that position during a routing operation (5–7 to 5–14). Any size of router may be used in inverted mode, although heavier routers are usually associated with this technique.

With the router attached securely, movement

INVERTED ROUTING WITH A ROUTER TABLE

5–7. A router table system designed to support a router in inverted mode. The tabletop is solid steel on a user-made wooden frame (also refer to 5–22).

5–8. The top may be raised to give access to the router for ease of cutter changing. Adjustable brackets make it possible to accommodate most router models.

5–9. Circular table inserts incorporate an eccentric locking system, applied by rotation. This insert, when fitted correctly, is level with the table—a desirable, but rare, feature.

(continued on following page)

INVERTED ROUTING WITH A ROUTER TABLE (CONTINUED)

5–10. The kit as supplied includes table, fence, sub-fences, and shims, plus micro-adjustment for the fence and magnetic dust chute. Details of a suitable stand are included for custom-making by the user.

5–11. Shims are used to pack out the sub-fences to create inequality between the in-feed and the out-feed sides on either side of the cutter. Naturally, the workpiece is reduced after passing the cutter, requiring, ideally, the out-feed side to extend by the reduced amount. The workpiece may then be pressed fully against both sides of the fence as the machining takes place.

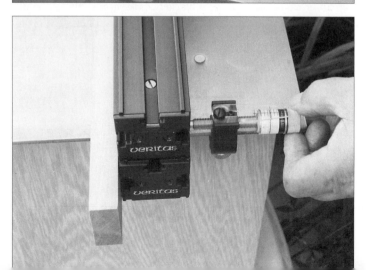

5–12. Micrometer adjustment of the fence setting is available with this special attachment.

(continued on following page)

INVERTED ROUTING WITH A ROUTER TABLE (CONTINUED)

5–13. Connected to a vacuum extractor, this dust chute is located behind the fence in line with the cutter orifice. It is infinitely relocatable, being magnetic.

5–14. By sliding the sub-fences towards the cutter as it revolves, a perfect fit is produced, ensuring excellent workpiece support, reducing tear-out, and directing dust to the extractor. The test piece is shown alongside the cutter.

of the workpiece to the cutter is a straightforward affair. Naturally, some means of controlling lateral cutting and its depth is essential, achievable by the addition of fences or guides of some

sort (5–15). Along with the routing table comes a whole catalog of add-ons, such as fences, hold-downs, miter fences, spacing shims, dust-extraction systems, table inserts, etc. Some systems

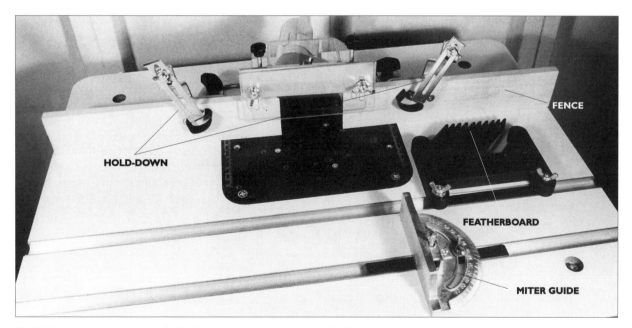

5–15. Fences, a miter guide, hold-downs, and a featherboard hold-in are all used at some time or another to ensure freedom of movement, but with control to prevent kickback and wandering.

include special attachments for specific routing operations. (Refer to Chapters 8 and 9.)

There are several possibilities to holding the router in this mode, including routing tables (5–16 to 5–21) (sometimes called routing benches), which can be either freestanding or bench-mounted. Of these, many are on offer by suppliers of routing accessories, including basic tabletops for which the user makes a suitable sub-frame (5–22). A standard Workmate bench or similar clamping device may be used as a sub-stitute routing table; such an arrangement has

ROUTER TABLES

5–16. A freestanding router table, rigid and substantial with an insert for attaching the router beneath the top.

5–17. A heavy-duty all-metal router table with hold-downs and adjustable fence.

5–18. Several practical features are characteristic of this model, including that of a lifting work top that gives access to the router.

SLIDING FENCE

5–19. Another unusual feature of this model is the sliding fence incorporating a clamping hold-down for workpiece security.

ROUTER TABLES (CONTINUED)

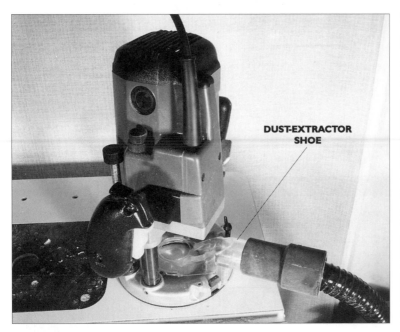

DUST-EXTRACTOR SHOE

5–20. *This router will be attached to the underside of the table in invert-ed mode, but it is shown on top of the table here, for photographic purposes, to illustrate the fitting of the dust extractor shoe.*

5–21. *A powerful vacuum extractor is connected to the dust shoe on the router (after the router is attached to the table). Virtually all the dust produced by the routing operation is extracted by this system.*

some appeal to the job-site worker who values its portability highly.

Router tables can be made from scratch, economically, by a competent and experienced woodworker, and there is much to be said for designing and custom-building such an important piece of equipment. Size and features can be built-in to suit the individual and take advantage of the particular workshop environment and the user's needs.

OVERHEAD ROUTING

This is not as easily achievable as inverted routing, because overhead routing requires a sturdy structure to suspend the machine over a worktable. A bracket or gantry to hold the router in

5–22. *Tabletops suitable for inverted routing are often available without bases. This is an example of a custom-built support made by the author.*

this position without deflection, and able to cope with the "on-off" effect generated by the routing operation, needs to be very rigid. Nevertheless, overhead routing is available and by various means, either by attaching the router to an existing machine as a "bolt-on" accessory or by attaching the router to a piece of equipment dedicated to routing in overhead mode (5–23 to 5–27).

Among the advantages of overhead routing are: clear visibility of the cutting action; readily accessible plunging function for control of cutting depth; and waste material is cleared more easily by dust extraction.

Fences, hold-downs, and other accessories associated with inverted routing are equally applicable to overhead routing but, in particular pin routing. (See the following page.)

OVERHEAD ROUTING

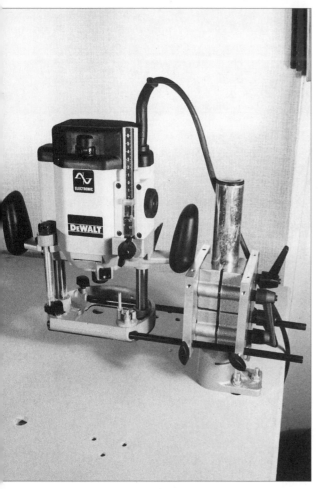

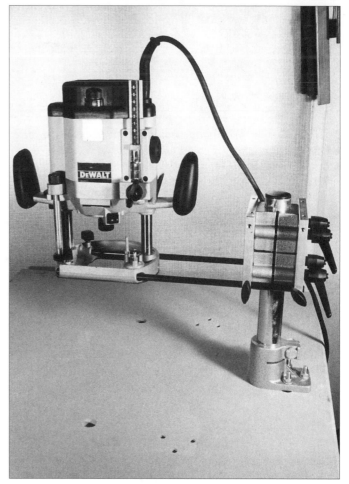

5–23. Here the router is in overhead mode, attached to equipment designed to accommodate the machine in many positions. The router is at its lowest position and close to the upright pillar on which it is supported.

5–24. Here the router is at its highest position and farthest from the pillar.

(continued on following page)

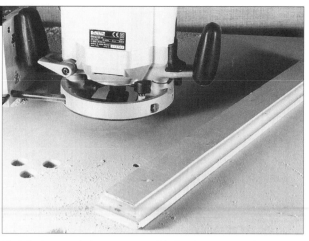

5–26. *A typical decorative molded edge produced by a bearing-guided cutter applied in overhead mode.*

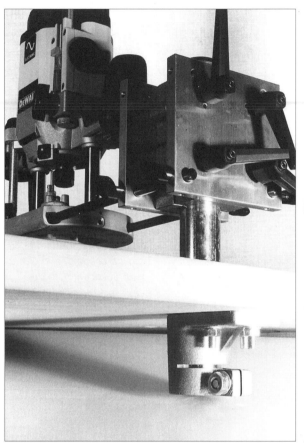

5–25. *By assembling the pillar bracket under the top of the workpiece, the router may be brought down onto the surface without impedance.*

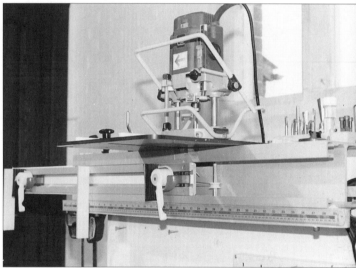

5–27. *This is a very flexible routing system with the router supported exclusively in overhead mode. Visibility during machining is a very desirable feature. Plunge bars fitted to the router for sophisticated depth control are another accessory from the same manufacturer.*

PIN ROUTING

With the router in overhead mode, a different application is possible using a captive pin inserted into the router table in line with and beneath the router spindle. The pin acts as a guide against which the workpiece is moved with its upper edge in contact with the cutter. An alternative is to attach the workpiece to a template that runs against the guide pin, thus producing a replica shape on the workpiece–provided that the pin and cutter are of the same diameter. By associating pins and guide bushes, it is possible to utilize the system very effectively, particularly for repetitive work or to produce very precise copies.

By definition, it might be claimed that the term "pin routing" would apply equally to the use of pin-ended cutters, discussed in Types of Cutter on pages 46 to 59. These may be used with some advantage in a router in overhead mode, allowing excellent visibility of the cutting action.

Several machines are made specifically for pin-routing operations, but they are generally large, freestanding affairs, immobile and relatively expensive—and aimed at the professional user.

HORIZONTAL ROUTING

This is a variation on inverted routing, but with the router lying on its side, its spindle horizontal, and the base of the router at right angles to the router table. Many operations are more practical in this mode, such as moldings on upper edges of panels (5–28 and 5–29). It may not always be possible to apply a freehand router to a panel edge, and with the router inverted the panel would then need to be held vertically while passing the cutter. In horizontal mode, with the workpiece passing underneath the cutter, the table acts as the fence. In this position, there is excellent visibility of the routing action, good waste clearance, and, more important, greater control of the workpiece.

5–28. With the router in horizontal mode, panels may be grooved or molded in either horizontal or vertical application. In this example, a cope-and-stick profiling operation is prepared.

5–29. Scribing the ends of a frame using the miter fence in the sliding groove. The workpiece has been clamped to the miter fence for added security.

6 Routing Principles and Techniques

Routing Speeds

Major variables involved in computing router speed as indicated by revolutions per minute are as follow:

1. Peripheral speed of cutter
2. Cutter diameter
3. Cutter profile
4. Depth of cut
5. Rate of feed

These variables are discussed in the following sections. The guidelines given for each may be adjusted as experience supplements knowledge.

PERIPHERAL SPEED AND CUTTER DIAMETER

It should be remembered (although it is rarely even mentioned) that with the router or any other machine that uses rotary cutters, it is the peripheral speed of the cutter that is of primary consideration and not simply its revolutions per minute. This may best be described as the speed at which an imaginary point on the edge of a cutter is revolving. It is usually expressed in feet per minute and is a term common to mechanical engineers and to the serious student of machining principles. Avoiding the intricacies of the topic, but examining its practical aspects with an example, consider two cutters, one ¼ inch in diameter, the other ten times bigger at 2½ inches in diameter. If these were rotating at 20,000

revolutions per minute (rpm), their respective peripheral speeds would be 1,300 and 13,000 feet per minute. As a matter of interest, the latter converts to 150 miles per hour!

If each revolution of the cutter removes a portion of material, obviously the larger-diameter cutter is capable of removing vastly more than the smaller. Equally this means that if it is not moving sufficiently quickly along the workpiece, it will be rubbing more than cutting, leading to burning of both workpiece and cutter due to the heat developed by the friction. Part of the equation for the operation is of course dependent on the depth of cut and the size of the cutter. A narrow slitting cutter has less tip area than a deep-molding type. All these things play their part when an appropriate speed of revolution is being selected.

A note about small-diameter cutters: They have small flutes, making for poor clearance of waste, so it is best to apply a slow feed rate in this case to avoid strain on the cutter.

CUTTER PROFILE

A straight cutter will remove less material in one revolution than a profiled one of the same diameter. This may be appreciated by taking the profile cutter and straightening it out. The straight cutter is obviously shorter and, therefore, the material with which it comes into contact per revolution is smaller in area. Logically, it is less stressed than the profile cutter and can, therefore, revolve at a faster cutting speed. Alternatively, the same speed of revolution might be used with the straight cutter but at a higher feed rate.

Router Speed and Feed-Rate Guidelines

As a general guide, Table 6–1 will help to select a suitable speed for cutters of certain diameters being used at moderate depths in softwood, hardwood, and man-made boards. Read all the instructions if they are stated by the cutter manufacturers and always err on the side of caution; that is, towards the lower speed, shallower depth of cut, and slower feed rate. If hardwood is being machined, however, it is best to use as fast a feed rate as possible in order to avoid the risk of overheating.

Direction of Feed

Feeding the router in the correct direction into the workpiece, or feeding the workpiece correctly towards a cutter, has very definite rules. Router users are frequently told to "feed the cutter into the material against its rotation" or "feed the workpiece against the rotation of the cutter." These techniques are shown in 6–1.

TABLE 6–1.

Cutter Diameter (Inches)	Router Speed (Revolutions Per Minute)
1/16 to 5/16	16,000 to 24,000
3/8 to 1	14,000 to 22,000
Over 1	*Larger Routers Only, 8,000 to 14,000

*Larger routers are 1¾ horsepower or greater

If the cutter is cutting a channel, then in whichever direction it moves, the cutter, being enclosed by the material, is subjected to the same cutting action. However, if only one side of the cutter is cutting, as in edge-shaping, then it should be the cutting edge that strikes the material as it revolves. Imagine the cutting edge to be a hook that is scooping out a path as it is moving forward. This tends to draw the cutter into the material, and is known as up-cutting. On the other hand, if the cutter were to be traveling in the opposite direction but still cutting on the same side of the cutter, the revolving cutting edge

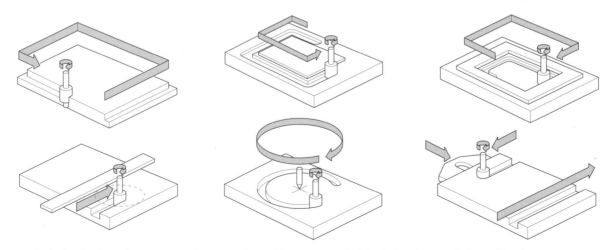

6–1. A selection of common routing operations with recommended feed directions, as indicated by the arrows.

would tend to push away, rather than to draw in, the material. This is known as down-cutting.

While, as a general rule, up-cutting should be applied to freehand routing, a router fixed in a frame or table can also be used. Especially useful to reduce splintering of hardwood workpieces or edge-crumbling with particleboard, down-cutting may be applied with advantage. Great care must be taken to resist the cutter's tendency to wander from the guide, so this is another case for making light cuts to avoid loss of control.

Routing Techniques

DRILLING

This section deals with conventional drilling, or boring, plus doweling, counterboring, and plug-cutting. The plunge router offers a great advantage over the power drill for this class of work. Its flat, sturdy base and smooth action allow controlled vertical penetration of the workpiece.

Conventional Drilling

Cutters made in the form of twist drills are available in diameters ranging from ⅛ to ½ inch (6–2). They may be made in either HSS (high-speed steel) or TCT (tungsten-carbide-tipped), the latter recommended especially for hard or abrasive materials.

Illus. 1–41 on page 30 shows a four-step procedure for drilling.

6–2. For fast drilling in open-grained materials and end grain in wood, the router drill bit is ideal. Slower speeds are advised for this tool.

Doweling

Dowel drills are intended for use in plunge routers in conjunction with jigs or fixtures dedicated to the accurate alignment of dowel holes. TCT lip- and spur-pattern cutters with slow spiral fluting (6–3), combined with speeds up to 22,000 rpm, ensure reliable drilling of small

SPUR

6–3. Lipped and spur-tipped router drill bit for accurate hole boring as needed for doweling applications.

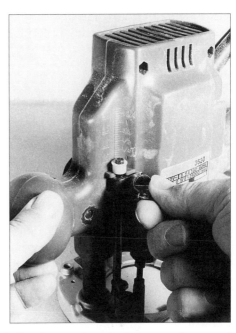

6–4. Depth control, a very important feature when doweling, is a simple matter with this clearly visible adjuster. Here the register shows alignment with the zero on the depth scale.

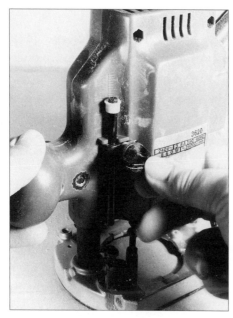

6–5. *Now the depth rod is raised to register with the ¾-inch line on the scale, meaning that when it reaches zero in a plunging movement it will have traveled ¾ inch.*

diameters. Accurate depths are often a consideration with this type of application, making depth control of the router an important facility (6–4 and 6–5).

Counterboring

Following the principle in which a screw head is to be sunk below the surface, after drilling for the insertion of the screw shank, the hole is opened to a bigger diameter to accept the screw head. Special counterbore drill cutters are made with two different diameters to meet the needs of the counterbored hole—but more efficiently by drilling and counterboring in one operation (6–6). To summarize, after the position required for the screw hole is marked on the workpiece, the router with the counterbore drill installed is located, ready for drilling. With the router preset to the required depth of the hole and counterbore, the drill may be brought down close to the surface to ensure its precise location.

This may be done with the router switched off until the operator is satisfied that all is well, following which the motor is switched on and the counterbore drilling operation is completed.

It is worth noting that a countersink drill using the same principle is available, but with a beveled bottom to suit a countersunk screw head.

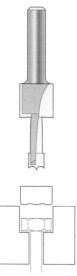

6–6. *An example of counterboring to house a bolt head. After fitting the bolt, it is possible to hide it by inserting a plug of appropriate diameter created by a plug cutter, as shown in 6–7.*

Plug-Cutting

To fill up holes left by screw heads or any other open hole that needs to be hidden, the plug cutter is the answer. There is a prerequisite that the plug must be a push-fit into the hole (6–7); therefore, some planning must be made for the respective diameters of plugs and counterbore screws. Just to be sure before commencing work on a masterpiece, it is wise to test the plug in some waste material similar in type to the workpiece. Usually, the holes to be plugged are bored into a long-grain surface rather than into the end grain. It follows that ideally the material for the plugs should be similar to the workpiece and taken from a part with a similar grain pattern. When the plugs are cut and prepared for insertion, the grain orientation should be noted in order to arrange a match as near as possible.

This is another application where the plunge router is superior to the power drill because of the security of the base and the router's action.

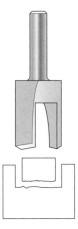

6–7. Plugs are used to fill holes left by screw heads or any other hole that needs to be hidden. Plug cutters, which are hollow in the center, can be used on routers to create a plug for insertion into a matching hole. After the cutter is applied, the plug is detached by applying a sideways force with a screwdriver.

STRAIGHT-LINE CUTTING

Perhaps the most common operation is straight-line cutting, whether for sizing, trimming, grooving, or decoration. Parallel routing in a straight line is an uncomplicated affair with the use of the side fence if routing freehand, or with a split fence on a routing table. In either of these examples—in which the edge of the workpiece acts as the guide—the straightness of the routed cut is dependent on the straightness of the edge (6–8 to 6–11). The cut will also be parallel to the edge of the workpiece. If an independent fence is used as a guide, it could be fixed to produce a straight line not necessarily parallel with the workpiece edge.

6–8. The Clamp 'N Tool Guide used is a quick clamping straightedge that has many practical uses. Setting it at a right angle is achieved here by the use of a traditional woodworker's try square.

6–9. Setting the clamp square may also be achieved with an adjustable angle setter. By this means, any angle could be set as required.

(continued on following page)

STRAIGHT-LINE CUTTING (CONTINUED)

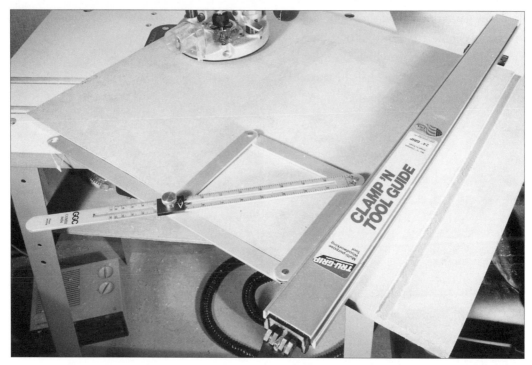

6–10. *An advanced angle setter allowing fine adjustments of any angle is shown here.*

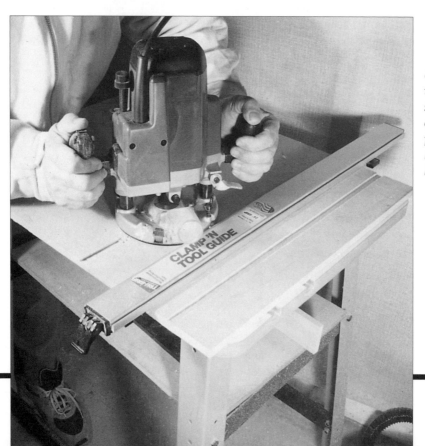

6–11. *Having set the clamp guide, straight-line routing can be performed freehand using the router base as a bearing guide.*

In passing: a groove is cut in the same direction as the grain; a dado is cut across the grain. Grooving and any other type of sawing or cutting that follows the direction of the grain may be referred to as rip cutting or rip sawing.

CROSSCUTTING

The term means cutting across the width, rather than along the length, of a workpiece (6–12), although it is still straight-line cutting of course. Often channels, dadoes, and dovetails need to be cut across members such as shelf sides and the like. Various basics need to be observed, including accurate separation and parallel routing, if crosscutting is to be repeated. The separation, or

6–12. These grooves were crosscut using a router attached to the radial-arm machine in overhead mode. Crosscutting was achieved by sliding the router on the overarm carriage.

divisions, of the routing is managed by either attaching fences at the required positions or by the use of equipment to which the router is attached (6–13).

Refer to Unicut Radial Arm Machine on page 128 for information on making crosscuts with routers and specialized machines.

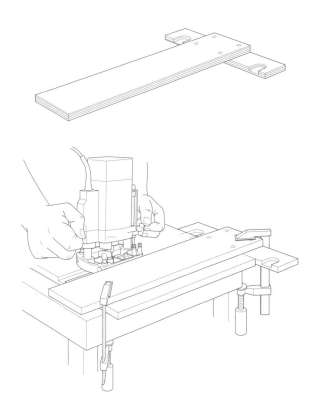

6–13. Top: A simple straight-line guide designed on the principle of the T-square. Below: By clamping the guide and workpiece to the bench, a secure routing procedure is effected, offering repetitive operations if required.

MORTISE-AND-TENON JOINT

One of the traditional joints produced by routing techniques is the mortise-and-tenon. This is a two-part joint. The mortise is a slot or hole cut into one piece, and the tenon is the mating piece that fits into the mortise. Methods for cutting each part are described on pages 102 and 103.

Cutting a Mortise

Several methods are available depending on the equipment and the experience of the operator. One of the most simple ways is with a guide bearing and a user-made template. The template consists of two pieces of board about ½ inch thick that are joined at a right angle. Into the top piece is a slot for the guide bearing cut to the size of the required mortise (6–14). (Refer to information on the use of guide bearings in Templates on pages 109 to 114.) To ensure correct location of the mortise, the workpiece and the template are aligned and both are then held in a suitable vise (6–15). Presuming the router has been fitted with the appropriate mortise cutter and guide, the routing of the mortise can be produced and reproduced as required.

Since the cutter produces a radiused end in the mortise slot (6–16), the matching tenon may be rounded at its ends to suit, or the mortise may be modified to fit the tenon by squaring the ends manually with a chisel (6–17).

Cutting a Tenon

Best produced on a router table with the machine in horizontal mode (refer to Horizontal Routing on page 94), the tenon may be cut by so-called "gang"-milling, that is, by clamping together a

CUTTING MORTISE-AND-TENON JOINTS

6–14 This basic mortise jig made from scrap plywood or MDF (medium-density fiberboard) can be used to cut the mortises. Refer to Chapter 4 for information on cutting MDF and plywood.

6–15. Here the mortise jig is arranged in place over the workpiece and clamped securely in a vise. The router is applied freehand with the appropriate mortise cutter.

6–16. Mortises produced this way have radiused ends, of course, left by the rotating cutter.

(continued on following page)

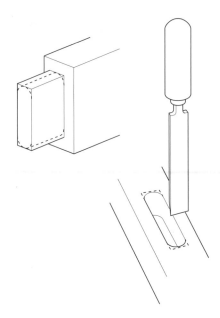

6–17. A choice must be made to either round the ends of a tenon to match the mortise or to square up the ends of the mortise to match the tenon.

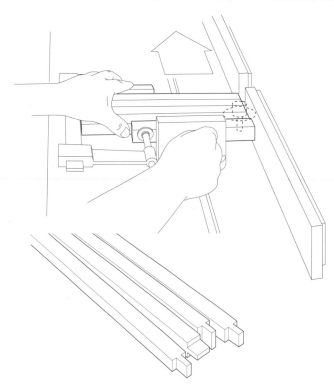

6–18. Using a clamp to hold a set of four workpieces (legs, for example), tenons may be machined on all of them simultaneously. This is an ideal situation for a router-table application.

number of pieces, say four legs, and routing them all in the same operation (6–18). One side of the tenon would be cut at a time.

DOVETAIL JOINT

Dovetail joints have been used by legions of woodworkers to join the sides and ends of boxes, drawers, and many kinds of cabinets. In the days when glues were not as durable or weatherproof as those we are fortunate to have today, joints that locked the members together were the hallmark of the carpenter and joiner. Dovetails made by hand indicate in the most immediate way the skill of the maker, and those made by the router operator may be as praiseworthy as those made by hand.

Jigs for cutting dovetails are available from many suppliers and one may believe they all work, but having said that, it is worth some investigation to establish which will best suit the individual in terms of practicality of use and flexibility of range (6–19 to 6–22).

Also refer to Woodrat Universal Routing Machine on pages 123 to 128 for information on cutting dovetails with a router and specialized machines.

TRIMMING

Taken literally, the term "trimming" may refer to adornment or ornamentation of some sort, but in routing applications it is taken to mean the removal of minor surplus waste that is attached to an otherwise finished member. In fact, it is usually the last routing action on a workpiece.

CUTTING DOVETAIL JOINTS WITH A JIG

6–19. *This dovetail cutter is designed to fit a jig intended exclusively for the production of dovetail joints.*

6–20. *This is the template used for guiding the dovetail cutter.*

6–21. *The template has been attached to the jig and the workpiece clamped in position. Now the routing of the dovetails can be performed by guiding the cutter with the template.*

6–22. *A typical example of a dovetail joint; both parts —pins and tails—are produced on the same jig.*

As mentioned in Self-Guiding Cutters on pages 48 and 49, bearing-guided cutters are ideal for trimming jobs. The bearing is only very slightly larger in diameter than the cutter to obviate the risk of scoring the surface with the cutter. Running the bearing along the workpiece or along a template means that anything overhanging will be trimmed off by the cutting action.

With a specially designed cutter, a similar application will produce a chamfer or bevel on the edge of the workpiece. These applications are ideal for the removal of overhang on surfaces treated with laminates or veneers.

Illus. 2–30 to 2–32 on page 52 show cutters that can be use in trimming applications. Illus. 7–3 and 7–4 on pages 110 and 112 show trimming applications involving the use of vacuum clamps and templates.

PANEL-RAISING

Panels intended to be framed must be reduced in thickness to match the grooves in the frame sides. In this respect, the term "raising" is something of a misnomer, because it is the relieving of the edge that creates the effect of the raised panel. A choice of cutter profiles is possible to

decorate the panel edge, but in principle the idea is to produce a panel to fill an aperture and keep it secure without straining the frame (6–23 and 6–24). One of the elements in the design is to

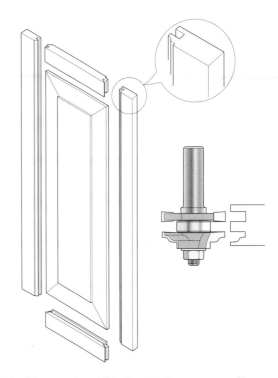

6–23. "Cope-and-stick" (otherwise known as profile-and-scribing) application using a combination cutter set, meant to be applied in two forms to create matching members of frames. Cutters and spacer are assembled on the shank in the order appropriate to whichever member is needed.

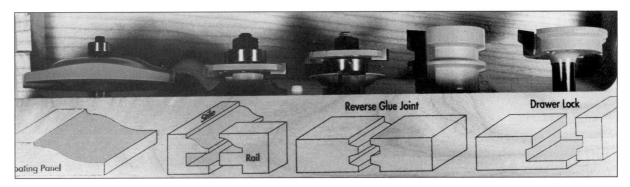

6–24. A useful set of cutters to gladden the heart of the kitchen cabinetmaker. These include a panel-raising cutter, cope-and-stick scribers, jointers, and a drawer-lock cutter.

make the edge fit tightly enough in the groove to avoid rattling but not so tight that it cannot move. The reason for this is that it's considered better not to glue this joint so as to allow room for movement of the panel as atmospheric conditions change, causing the panel to expand and contract.

Routing of panel edges may be achieved by a router fixed in inverted, horizontal, or overhead mode. Because of the size of the cutter—up to 3½ inches in diameter—only a heavy-duty router is viable and freehand routing is not recommended.

EDGE TREATMENTS

Edge treatments—shapes or decorations made to the edges of boards—are as widely diverse as ever, except that with the router the home craftsman can simulate the work that used to require the expertise associated with old-time craftsmen or the demanding skills of shaper operators.

Fixed routers in inverted or overhead mode are essential for this operation, since it most often means the use of large cutters with complex profiles. (Refer to Inverted and Overhead Routing on pages 87 to 92.) A short list of areas suitable for edge treatments includes handrails, picture frames, shelves, panels, and many other items constructed of standard joinery.

The type of cutter necessary for molding is ideally suited for ball-bearing guidance, which is generally fitted on the end of the cutter (6–25). The workpiece usually has a straight, flat element in its design that functions perfectly as the register and guide against which the cutter bearing will glide as the cutter does its work.

Sometimes it is necessary to combine two operations with different cutters producing profiles that merge to create a required shape as, for instance, handrails.

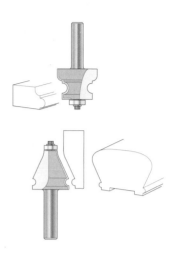

6–25. For fixed-router operations, either in inverted or overhead mode, bearing-guided cutters are very suitable for the production of domestic moldings—as shown in these examples.

FLUTES, BEADS, AND REEDS

Flutes, beads, and reeds are decorative moldings used on furniture. Flutes are rounded parallel grooves. Beads are projecting molding. Reeds are semi-cylindrical parallel elements. These applications may be treated similarly (6–26 to 6–30). Cutters may feature just one ele-

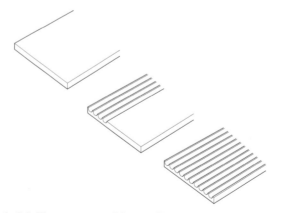

6–26. Three stages of fluting. Shown are a plain board prepared with flat, straight faces and edges; the board partially fluted; and finally, the board with a completely fluted face. Similar principles to fluting apply to reeding and beading operations, using appropriate cutters.

ment, such as a radius for cutting a single bead, and this may be applied repeatedly, such as when making parallel cuts to decorate an edge molding. To achieve the same result in one pass, cutters are made with multiple bead shapes. Combined shapes of internal and external radii are available to allow a range of beads and reeds to be machined from one cutter (6–31).

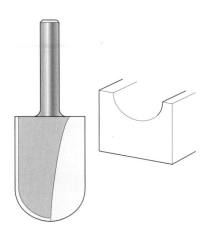

6–27. *A cutter with a round nose, suitable for a fluting operation.*

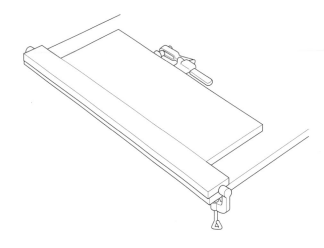

6–28 *Clamping of the workpiece in readiness for fluting, with all clamping devices lower than the work surface.*

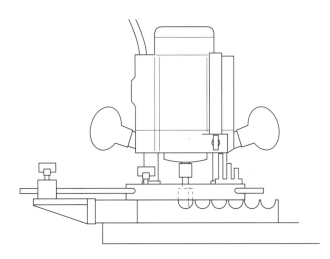

6–29. *Cross-section view of the fluting setup that shows the depth of the cutter and the fence fitted to the router base. The edge of the workpiece acts as a reference for each pass of the cutter, ensuring that the flutes are parallel.*

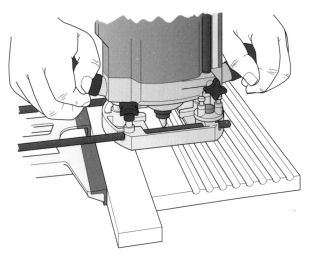

6–30. *The fluting operation in progress. Each pass of the router is adjusted by resetting the fence to locate correct spacing of the flutes.*

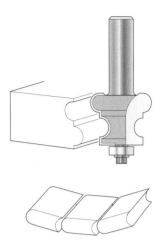

6–31. Matching members that require engaging profiles, as in the example of tambour tops or similar items, may be obtained from one cutter, as shown.

All of these decorative effects may be applied to curved or straight pieces and, providing the cutters are relatively small and suitable for use in a small router, it is possible to operate it freehand.

INLAYING

Preparing recesses for inlaying is appropriate for routing, whether for the insertion of a hinge or other cabinet hardware, for example, or for a wood-to-wood application as inlaid stringing. Cutters with side- and end-cutting features are best; in the case of a shallow but wide recess, a cutter as wide as possible is then practical—a possibility being to acquire a cutter to match in width the piece that is to be inlaid. This consideration is also valid if a channel is being prepared to accept a decorative line or "string," as it is often called. Lightweight routers can be a great asset for this type of work, particularly if a pattern is being followed using a freehand technique.

Recesses may also be made using a bearing-guided side cutter (6–32). The bearing can be changed to cut different preset depths. A typical set would include a cutter with three bearings that are ¼, ½, and ¾ inch in diameter.

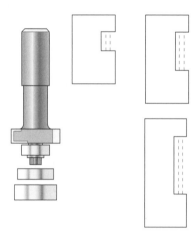

6–32. This inlaying-cutter assembly can create recesses of different depths and heights. Included in the set are bearings of different diameters.

CHAPTER **7** **Templates**

Templates, which are also referred to as patterns among router users, guide the router so that it can cut a particular shape. The template is placed onto or under the workpiece, and the router is used to duplicate the template's profile.

Why use templates? They are useful when making repetitive shapes. Taking a hypothetical project as an example, suppose it is necessary to produce a set of children's table mats from some attractive veneered plywood (7–1). Assuming the mats are to be shaped like a rabbit, a template will be cut to the desired shape. A piece of scrap plywood or mdf (medium-density fiberboard) will do fine, as long as it is clean and smooth on both faces. Any convenient means will do to cut the pattern: a scroll saw or coping saw, for instance. It is best to smooth all the edges and corners around the periphery of the template because it will be used as a pilot to run against the bearing guide on the cutter. In this case, the

USING TEMPLATES TO PRODUCE TABLE MATS

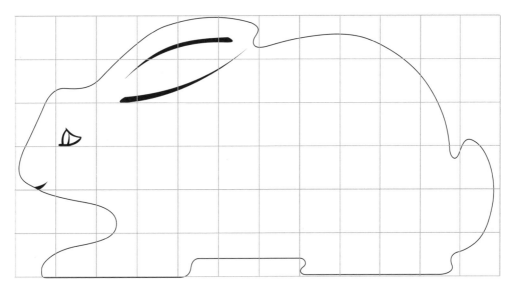

7–1. A template for a child's table mat made from plywood or MDF (1 inch squares).

(continued on following page)

USING TEMPLATES TO PRODUCE TABLE MATS (CONTINUED)

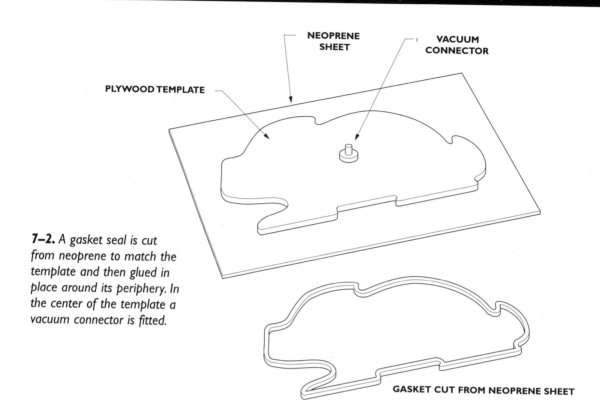

NEOPRENE SHEET

VACUUM CONNECTOR

PLYWOOD TEMPLATE

7–2. *A gasket seal is cut from neoprene to match the template and then glued in place around its periphery. In the center of the template a vacuum connector is fitted.*

GASKET CUT FROM NEOPRENE SHEET

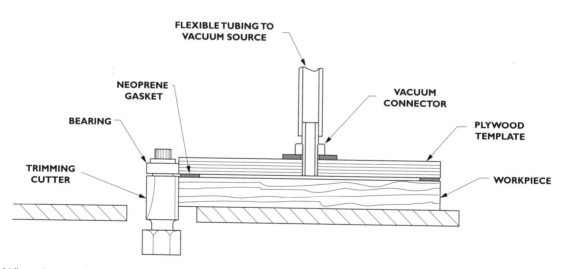

FLEXIBLE TUBING TO VACUUM SOURCE

NEOPRENE GASKET

BEARING

VACUUM CONNECTOR

PLYWOOD TEMPLATE

TRIMMING CUTTER

WORKPIECE

7–3. *When the template is placed on the workpiece or blank and vacuum pressure is applied, sufficient clamping is applied to hold both parts together for the routing of superfluous waste from the workpiece with a bearing-guided cutter. This is a suitable application for an inverted router in a routing table.*

cutter and its bearing have identical diameters, say, ¾ inch. It is necessary to prepare the plywood mats prior to applying the routing process. These pieces will be called "blanks" and as many as are required will be cut roughly to size, but slightly over–say, ⅛ inch bigger—all around.

A decision has to be made about the means by which the template and blank will be stuck together (7–2 and 7–3). Because the entire template has to lie flat on the router table and router, it is not possible to use a clamp to temporarily attach the template and blank. In this case, double-sided adhesive tape will be sufficient. Apply the tape to either the template or the blank and peel off its protective backing. Align the two parts carefully to see that the blank overhangs equally all around the template. Bring the template and blank together and give them a squeeze in a vise or with a clamp, to firm up the bond. Test to see that they have no tendency to slide apart under side pressure. Assuming that the two parts may now be handled as a unit, it may be called the workpiece. The router should be set up ready for use in a router table, the cutter projecting through the table insert.

The next step involves trimming the template. Trimming in this mode means projecting the cutter to just fully expose its bearing above the table, in order to make contact with the template but not the workpiece. This means that if the bearing is in contact with the template, the cutter is in contact with the blank. Therefore, any surplus material will be cut from the blank as the template is steered around in contact with the bearing. Obviously the operator must be alert when placing the workpiece because if it is placed upside down, the blank will make contact with the bearing. There is no hazard, only a waste of time, because the cutter will not make contact with the blank.

Having trimmed the entire blank and removed it from the template, usually it is enough to slide a blunt knife between the two parts in order to release the grip of the tape and smooth any remaining sharp corners. The mat is now finished. Repeat the process for as many copies as are required.

Template Applications

Templates may be used in the following ways:

1. Attached to the top or underside of the blank.
2. Attached to the blank by various means— adhesive tape, nails, screws, regular and vacuum clamping (refer to 7–2 and 7–3)— depending on the type of material and its shape.
3. Internally (7–4), when the cutter is following the inside periphery of an aperture.
4. Externally, when the cutter is following the outside periphery of a pattern (7–4).

Users are well advised when routing with templates to check, as with every operation, the feed direction. This is the direction the cutter is moved relative to the material, or vice versa. More information is given on this important subject in Chapter 6.

Guide Bushes

Guide bushes (7–5 and 7–6) have a function similar to the bearings fitted on self-guiding cutters, except that the latter may be applied directly to a workpiece edge and not necessarily with a template. Guide bushes are most frequently found in combination with template guides or special-purpose jigs. Sizes of guide bushes range from ¼ to 2 inches in inside diameter. Clearly, the guide-bush hole must be

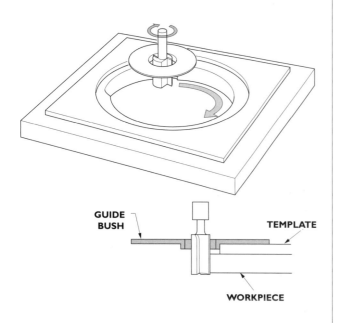

7–5. *Cutters project through guide bushes that may be attached to the base of the router. Guide bushes are intended to follow the shape of a template or jig, permitting the cutter to shape the workpiece.*

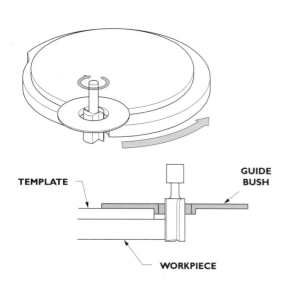

7–4 (Top). *Template used internally, so the cutter follows the inside periphery of the pattern.* **(Bottom).** *Template used externally, so the cutter follows the outside periphery of the pattern. Feed direction must be considered carefully in all applications.*

7–6. *On the left, the guide bush is fitted into a sub-base, but on the right the bush fits directly onto the router base.*

bigger in diameter than the cutter. In principle, the guide bush is attached by screws to the router base; the cutter, held as usual in the collet, projects through the hole in the guide. Normal plain cutters are applicable to guide-bush operations with allowance made for the difference in their respective diameters (7–7). This difference is referred to as "offset." For instance, if a cutter of ½-inch diameter is used with a guide bush of ¾-inch diameter, the difference in their diameters is ¼ inch. To calculate the offset, divide the difference by 2; in this example, the answer is ⅛ inch. Therefore, when laying out a template for use with this setup, there must be ⅛ inch added to the sides of an internal template, or ⅛ inch subtracted from the sides of an external template in order to correctly rout the required size.

Fitting the guide bush is a simple matter, most router manufacturers offering their own guiding systems to suit their own products. Guide bush-es come with a flange pierced to receive a couple of screws for attachment to the router base. A typical system would include a set of 10 or 12 guide bushes with flanges drilled to a specification suitable for a particular router.

Pilot Bearings

As mentioned in Self-Guiding Cutters on pages 48 and 49, pilot bearings—or ball bearings, to give them their general name—are frequently used in conjunction with templates. Several variables are possible with pilot bearings; for example, if the bearing is changed for another of a different diameter, the cutter will cut to a different depth. This can offer the possibility of stocking fewer cutters with a reduction in cost and storage. In addition, it allows the cutting of deep profiles to be accomplished in stages, rather than risking an uncontrolled grab of more material than is safe or other damage to the equipment.

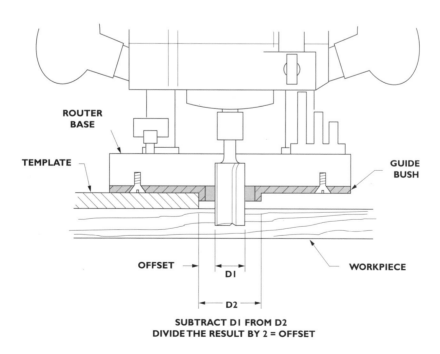

ROUTER BASE

TEMPLATE

GUIDE BUSH

WORKPIECE

OFFSET

D1

D2

SUBTRACT D1 FROM D2
DIVIDE THE RESULT BY 2 = OFFSET

7–7. Calculating guide-bush "offset" when using templates.

Pilot bearings may be mounted on the shank above, or on the end of, the cutter, each method having advantages depending on the routing application (7–8).

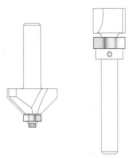

7–8. Bearings may be fitted at the end of a cutter, as shown on the left, or above the cutter on the shank. The bearing diameter also controls the depth of cut and in some cases may be interchangeable to provide cuts of variable depth.

Part of the routing equation may still include whether the router is used freehand or fixed in overhead or inverted mode. Permutations of variation are enormous and these will expand and develop as the user becomes more experienced, but here are a few examples of template use with a pilot-bearing cutter:

1. Freehand with bearing on shank
2. Freehand with end-bearing
3. Router fixed and inverted with bearing on shank
4. Router fixed and inverted with end-bearing
5. Router fixed in overhead mode with bearing on shank
6. Router fixed in overhead mode with end-bearing

8 Special-Purpose Machines

Turning

It is safe to assume that to a woodworker the word "turning" refers to work produced on a lathe. Essentially, any shaping of wood by rotating it while applying a cutting tool of some sort may be called turning. Illus. 8–1 to 8–6 show a machine to which a router can be attached to create decorative carvings and a sample of such carvings.

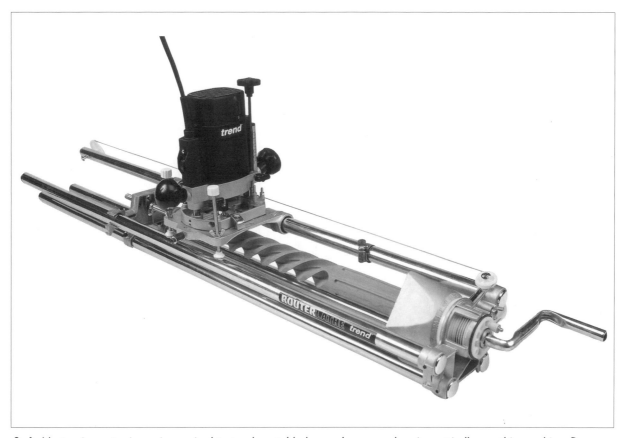

8–1. No turning experience is required to produce table legs, columns, and various spindles on this machine. Decorative carvings similar to turnings, as shown in 8–2 to 8–6, may be produced, and in many cases these are of such quality as to be almost impossible on a conventional lathe.

8–2   8–3   8–4   8–5   8–6

8–2 to 8–6. *A sample of the carvings that can be produced using the machine shown in 8–1.*

A typical router turning system might comprise a headstock to hold and rotate the workpiece and a sliding carriage to support the router (8–7). By rotating the workpiece in the headstock as the router is traversed along the carriage bars, it is possible to create spindles similar to conventional turned work (8–8 to 8–11). Additionally, it is possible to machine the spindle along its length by keeping it stationary and running the router along the bars to cut flutes, grooves, or other decorations. An index system incorporated in the headstock provides the facility to cut equally spaced grooves around the workpiece.

Applications on parallel or tapered cylinders include straight beads and reeds, left- and right-hand spirals or grooves, and collars around the workpiece. With a suitable attachment it is possible to fit a template alongside the carriage bars to guide the router for repeat shaping.

ROUTER TURNING SYSTEM

8–7. *A conventional twin-bar lathe set up for normal turning.*

(continued on following page)

8–8. A workpiece is attached between the headstock and tailstock. The router carrier is fitted onto
the bed bars of the lathe.

8–9. Routing of grooves is carried out along the length of the
workpiece.

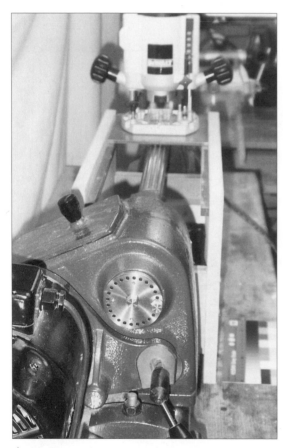

8–10. The workpiece is rotated as grooves are
machined along its surface. The indexing ring at the
end of the spindle is used to locate the workpiece
for equally divided grooves.

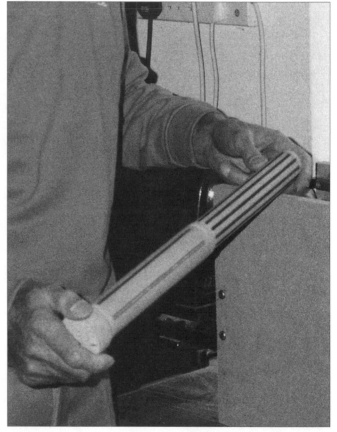

8–11. A sample of work with grooves produced by this method
and inlaid with contrasting decorations.

Joint-Making Machines

Numerous joints may be made by machines that either hold the router for hand-applied workpieces or machines to which the workpiece is secured and the router applied. Three such machines are described in this section.

ROUTERACK ROUTING SYSTEM

More than just another routing table, the Routerack system will support a router in inverted mode for molding, strip-forming, and edgework (8–12 to 8–22). Scribing edges for cope-and-stick (stile-and-rail) applications can be

CUTTING CHAMFERS WITH THE ROUTERACK ROUTER SYSTEM

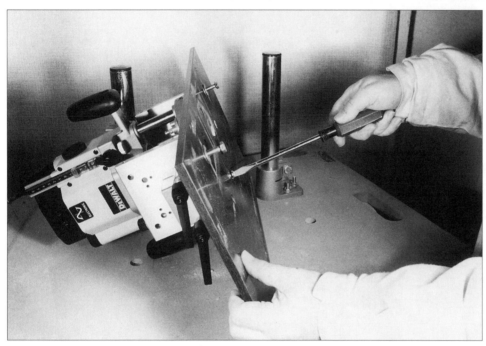

8–12. The Routerack is a system providing a multiplicity of routing modes whose basis depends on the securing of the router to the work top.

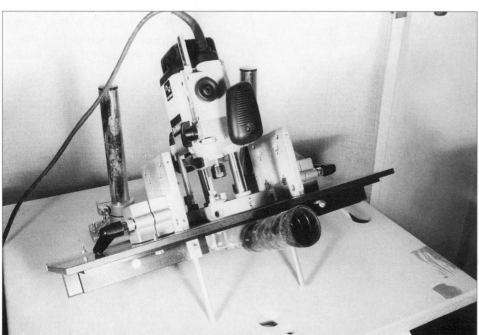

8–13. Here the unit is inverted to show the brackets and mounting plates used to connect the work top to the pillars.

(continued on following page)

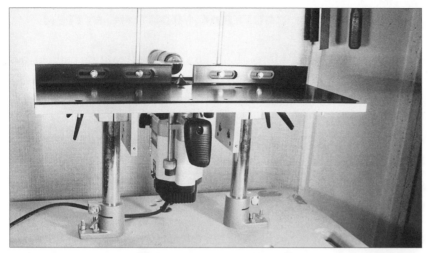

8–14. Mounted in inverted mode, the router is attached to the work top and suspended above the workbench. A fence and dust-extraction chute are added.

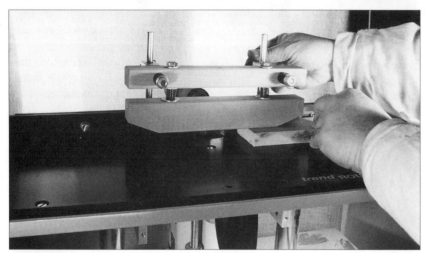

8–15. Spring-loaded hold-downs are adjusted to give firm contact to prevent the workpiece from rising, but not too great a pressure to prevent its movement across the cutter.

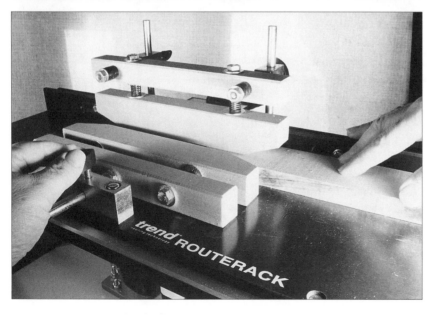

8–16. Horizontal hold-downs are also attachable to prevent sideways wandering of the workpiece.

(continued on following page)

produced with the addition of a miter fence. With the router in overhead mode, many machining operations are available, including profiling; and, with a beam attached, trammel work is possible. Panel-raising, edge-molding, and similar opera-tions may be undertaken with the router set up in horizontal mode.

Accessories of this type can be acquired a little at a time, adding attachments as and when required.

CUTTING CHAMFERS WITH THE ROUTERACK ROUTER SYSTEM (CONTINUED)

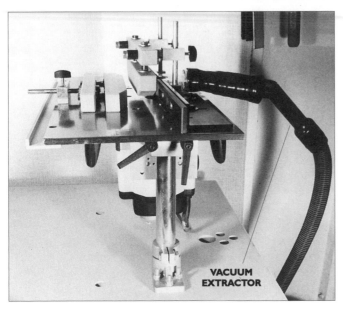

8–17. A powerful vacuum extractor is connected to the dust chute incorporated in the fence assembly. This extraction sys-tem is very effective.

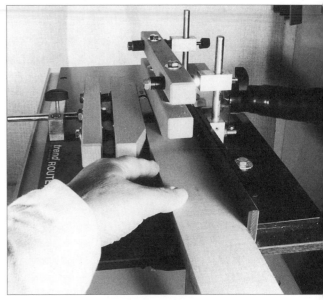

8–18. A bevel cutter has been installed to produce a chamfer along the edge of the workpiece. Both hold-downs are set correctly and the vacuum extractor activated; routing can proceed.

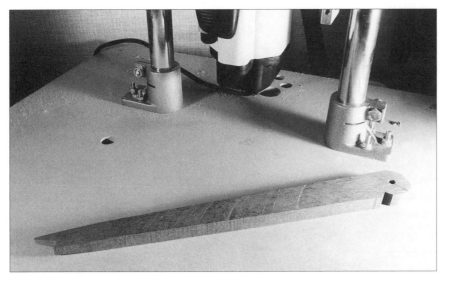

8–19. Ready at hand is a user-made push stick, essen-tial to most routing applica-tions that involve control of a moving workpiece.

(continued on following page)

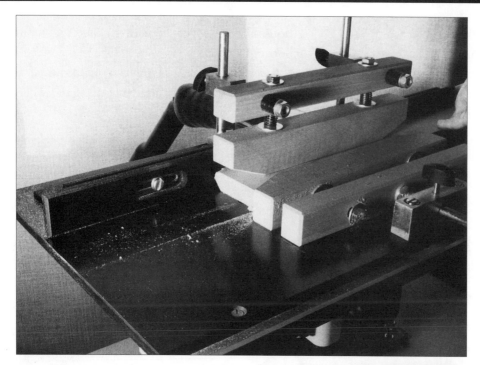

8–20. *Little dust is escaping from the system and the heavy-duty router cuts the chamfer in one pass.*

8–21. *Near the end of the operation the push stick is applied for safety.*

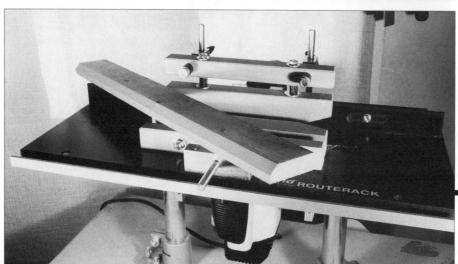

8–22. *A perfect chamfer and finish with little or no dust from the operation. The workpiece was MDF (medium-density fiberboard.)*

WOODRAT UNIVERSAL ROUTING MACHINE

The Woodrat is a unique universal routing machine capable, in this writer's opinion, of performing more woodworking operations than any other. This is due to the functions of its movable elements, which comprise a sliding clamp to accommodate the workpiece combined with a sliding carriage that supports the router (8–23 to 8–31). Add the plunging facility of the router and the owner has a veritable woodworking machine shop within the spread of both hands.

Routing in the overhead mode is a feature of the Woodrat, providing clear visibility of the cutter and workpiece during the machining process. Rapid action and accuracy are part of the attraction of this equipment, together with a sense of involvement from the operator.

WOODRAT ROUTING SYSTEM COMPONENTS

8–23. *Components of the Woodrat—an advanced routing system using a sliding carriage to which a router is attached. Clamps hold the workpiece while machining is performed.*

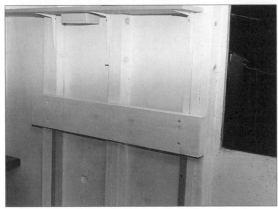

8–24. *A wall plate is attached securely to the wall of the workshop to receive the machine.*

8–25. *Plunge bars are fitted to the router to facilitate simplified and effective depth control.*

(continued on following page)

WOODRAT ROUTING SYSTEM COMPONENTS (CONTINUED)

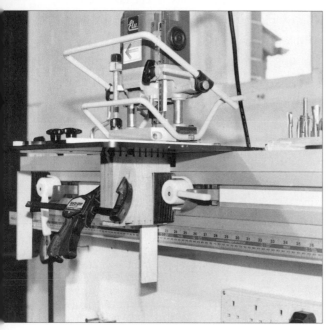

8–26. *The Woodrat set up for cutting dovetails in several components simultaneously.*

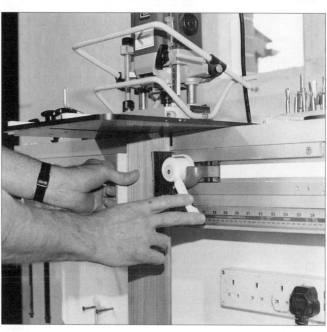

8–27. *Clamping of the workpiece is swift and positive using the cam-clamp system.*

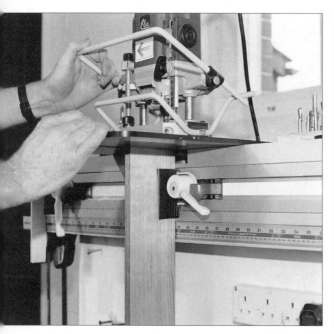

8–28. *Using the plunge bars to set the depth for cutting the dovetails.*

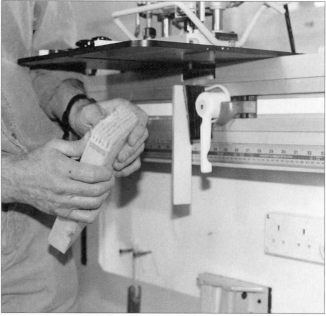

8–29. *An ordinary scrubbing brush is attached to the end of a clamping board to provide firm pressure without damage to the workpiece.*

(continued on following page)

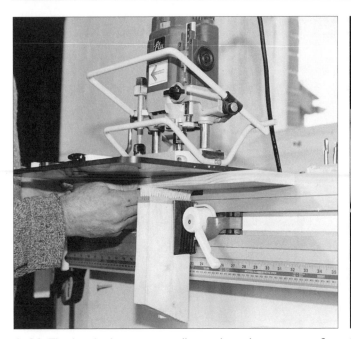

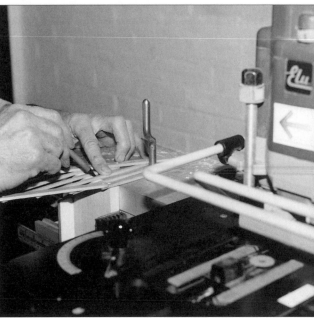

8–30. The brush clamp in use, allowing lateral movement of the workpiece as routing is carried out.

8–31. A practical method of marking equally divided portions of a workpiece is possible by the application of a simple attachment.

The system offers the opportunity to produce joints on workpieces as large as a dining table or as small as a dolls' house. Every variation of dovetails is possible (8–32 to 8–39), including compound angles and variable spacing. While an inexhaustible variety of joints may be produced on the Woodrat, it functions with a relatively small collection of cutters. Some user-made jigs may be added to extend the function of the equipment, and these are clearly detailed by the manufacturer.

CUTTING DOVETAILS WITH THE WOODRAT ROUTING SYSTEM

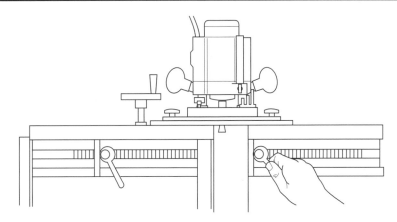

8–32. A test piece is clamped in the right-hand clamp and the router is slid on its carriage to cut a sample dovetail.

(continued on following page)

CUTTING DOVETAILS WITH THE WOODRAT ROUTING SYSTEM (CONTINUED)

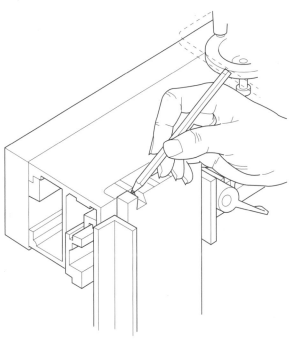

8–33. *The test piece is transferred to the left-hand clamp and the outline of the tail part of the dovetail is marked on the clamping face.*

8–34. *The tail mark. This mark is then used to align the component to receive the pins. At the other end of the channel, the component to receive the tails will be clamped.*

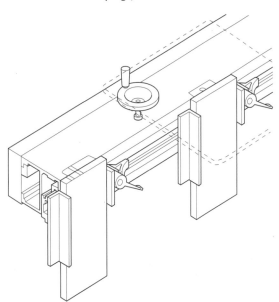

8–35. *With the "pin" workpiece clamped in the left clamp and the "tail" workpiece clamped in the right, both workpieces move simultaneously.*

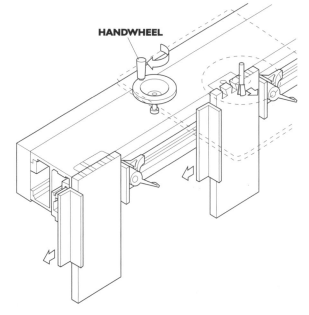

8–36. *The carriage is moved by winding the hand-wheel as shown, aligning first the pins with the marks to cut the tails.*

(continued on following page)

CUTTING DOVETAILS WITH THE WOODRAT ROUTING SYSTEM (CONTINUED)

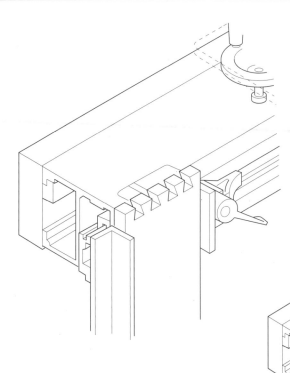

8–37. Now the tail workpiece is transferred to the left-hand clamp and the pins clamped in the right-hand clamp. The plate on which the router is mounted is set at an angle to suit the type of dovetails being made.

8–38. As each tail is aligned with the mark on the left, its corresponding pin may be cut on the right-hand workpiece.

8–39. An assortment of just a few examples of joints that can be made on the Woodrat. Notice the dovetail joints on the right.

UNICUT RADIAL-ARM MACHINE

Similar in concept to the radial-arm saw, the Unicut provides a means of supporting a router (or a portable power saw, or an angle grinder) for either fixed overhead routing or for traverse-cutting on the sliding carriage (8–40 to 8–42).

8–40. A radial-arm machine designed to accept bolt-on power tools. The overhead arm swings radially to permit crosscutting of miters and bevels.

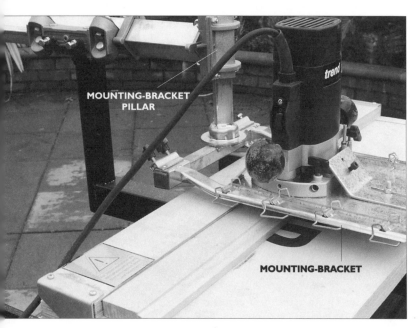

8–41. In the overhead mode with the router fixed on its mounting bracket, edge-molding is a simple matter. Depth control is available by raising or lowering the mounting bracket pillar.

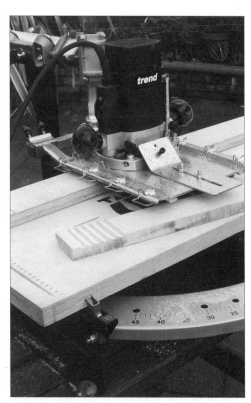

8–42. Crosscutting of grooves and other similar cuts is performed by sliding the router on the overarm carriage.

CHAPTER **9**

Jigs and Fixtures

A jig guides cutters and a fixture holds a workpiece. These simplified definitions are used to show the fundamental difference between the two devices. Some routing accessories combine the two as found in the Woodrat, described in Joint-Making Machines on pages 119 to 128.

Miscellaneous Jigs

Several types of commercial jig are available, made to solve the problems of routing joints found in domestic joinery, such as kitchen countertops, staircase housing, letter boxes, hinge-fitting, etc. For a given jig, a guide bush is matched and fitted to the router with the correct cutter installed. The operation may be achieved by clamping the jig to the workpiece in the required position and applying the guided cutter to the slotted jig.

There are many types of jig available to perform various routing functions. The illustrations and captions in this chapter show and describe many of these jigs.

Many items of furniture are elliptical, like tables and mirror frames. Certain jigs are available offering adjustable facility to allow the cutting or molding of any size of circle and ellipse within the limits of the trammel bars on which the router is supported

One such device is the pivot frame jig shown in 9–2 to 9–7, which has a wide range of uses, including cutting circles and rings and, when used as a trammel, to mold circular edges. The ellipse jig shown in 9–8 to 9–11 can also produce circles and ellipses that are used in woodworking projects.

Other jigs featured in this chapter include those used to aid in relief and incised carving (9–1 and 9–12 to 9–18), those that can be used to route letters in signs (9–19), and those that can be used to make joints and other cuts (9–20 to 9–22).

Dovetail Jigs

In general, all dovetail jigs operate on the same principle, comprising a frame with attached "finger" guides, to which may be clamped the workpieces for the cutting of both tails and pins (9–23 to 9–27). Cutters, made from HSS and TCT and designed to match the jigs, come ready-shaped to produce both tails and pins. Guide bushes are used to pilot the cutters around the template fingers, and the elements combined in the system ensure accurate size and spacing of the joining members (9–28 to 9–30).

Dovetails can also be produced on a jointing apparatus that incorporates a sliding carriage, such as the Woodrat described on pages 123 to 127 in Chapter 8. An immediate advantage with this machine is the possibility, once having set it up correctly, of cutting several tails simultaneously (9–31).

JIG FOR SURFACE-ROUTING APPLICATIONS

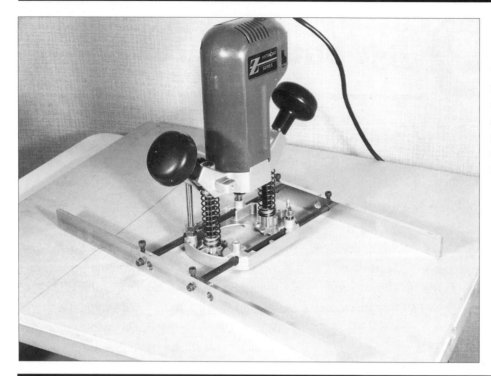

9–1. In this example, the side fence has been exchanged for twin ski bars to act as a support for the router in surface applications such as relief carving.

PIVOT-FRAME JIG

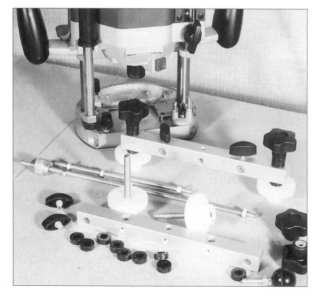

9–2. These components are assembled and attached to the router to make up a pivot frame unit.

9–3. In principle the pivot frame cuts circles, rings, and scalloped designs.

(continued on following page)

PIVOT-FRAME JIG (CONTINUED)

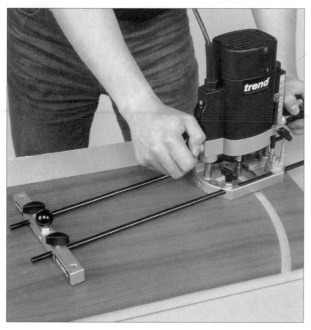

9–4. The pivot frame may also be used as a trammel for molding circular edges or as a ski frame for surface work.

9–5. The pivot-frame jig in a circle-cutting application.

9–6 and 9–7. Examples of the types of decorative element that can be produced with the pivot-frame jig.

ELLIPSE JIG

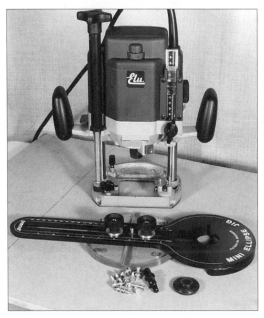

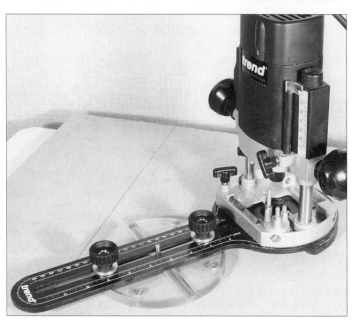

9–8. These components are assembled and attached to the base of the router, with which they combine to make up an ellipse jig.

9–9. An ellipse jig provides a practical method for the production of the ellipses and circles that might be used in frames, clocks, and small tables.

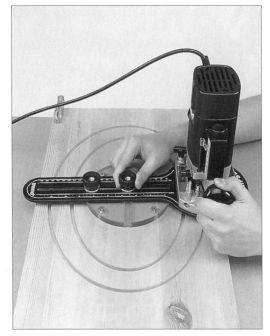

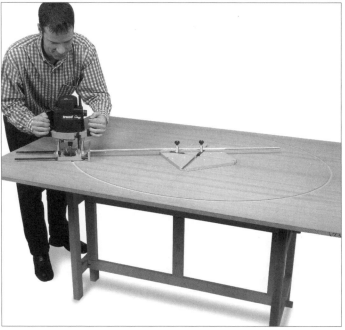

9–10. An ellipse jig being used in a circle-cutting application.

9–11. Here the jig is being used as a trammel to cut out a large circle.

INCISED CARVING WITH TEMPLATE JIGS

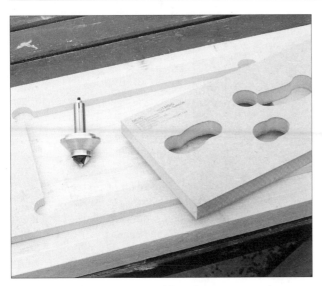

9–12. Incised carving is possible using one cutter in a plunge router and special template designs. The cutter is a V shape with a bearing-mounted circular guide fitted above it on the shank.

9–13. A template is installed in a frame and mounted on the workpiece.

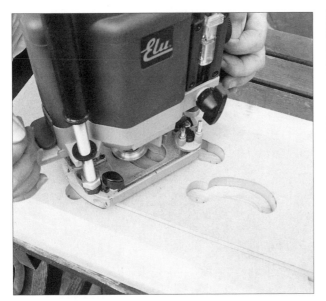

9–14. Routing is commenced guided by the template with cutting depths varying according to the width of the apertures. This creates deeper, wider elements as required by the design.

9–15. The template is reversed in the frame and routed as before. Then it is turned over and the process repeated. A second template is added and the sequence of cuts repeated.

(continued on following page)

INCISED CARVING WITH TEMPLATE JIGS

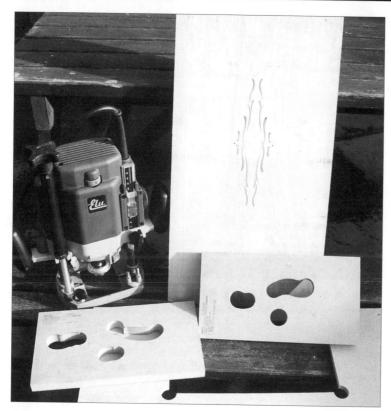

9–16 to 9–18. When the process is completed the result is a graceful combination of curved lines, varying in depth and width with the look of hand-carving.

9–17.

9–18.

LETTER-ROUTING JIG

9–19. *This jig can be used to rout lettering in signs.*

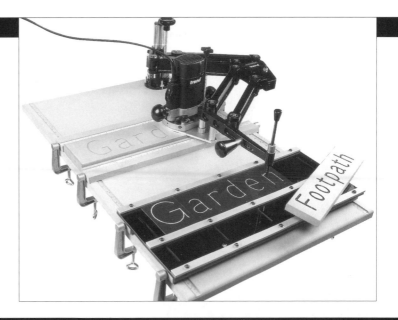

COMBINATION JIG

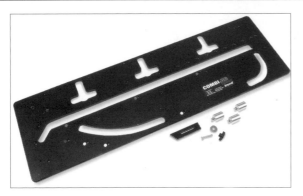

9–20. *A whole range of joints and cuts are available with the combination jig. The principle is combining a guide bush and cutter in a template prepared specially to produce kitchen cabinet-top joints.*

9–21. *The guide-bush assembly attaches to the router base.*

9–22. *The router applied to the template and being guided to produce slots, grooves, and other cuts.*

DOVETAIL JIG

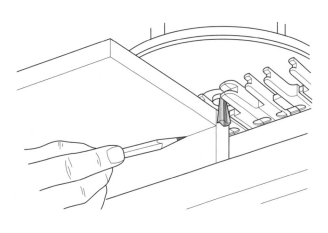

9–23. *Having marked the thickness of the material from the workpiece, the dovetail cutter is set to this depth.*

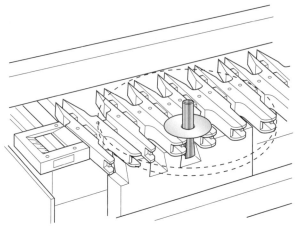

9–24. *The cutter, guided by the bush in the guide fingers, cuts the tails.*

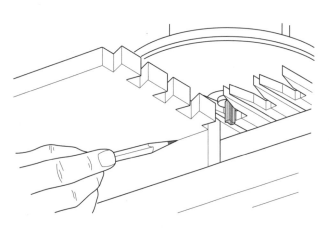

9–25. *After the tails are cut, the assembly is rotated and the pin workpiece is clamped in the jig, using the tail member to mark the required depth of cut.*

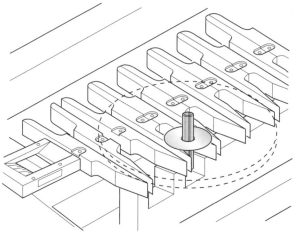

9–26. *Following the guide fingers with the bush, the cutter removes waste to shape the pins.*

(continued on following page)

DOVETAIL JIG (CONTINUED)

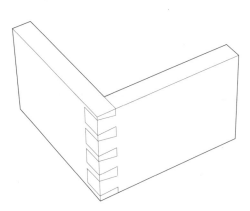

9–27. Some practice may be necessary to produce a perfect fit, but it is achievable if the instructions are followed as given by the manufacturer.

9–28. A guide bush and dovetail cutter installed in the router in preparation for application to the Leigh Dovetail Jig.

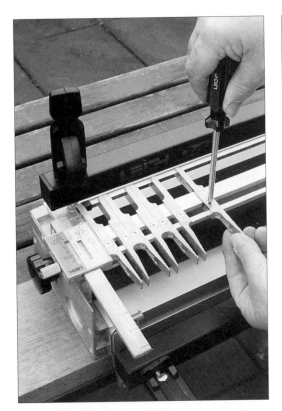

9–30. Removal and rotation of the finger assembly is all that is necessary to change from cutting pins to tails to complete the dovetail joints.

9–29. Adjustment of guide fingers is carried out on the jig frame to create the desired widths of pins and tails.

WOODRAT DOVETAIL-CUTTING MACHINE

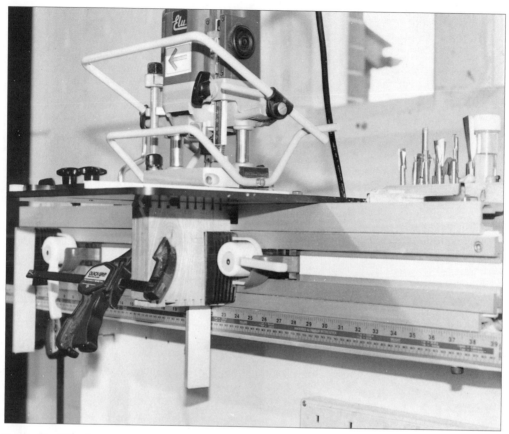

9–31. The Woodrat is a special-purpose machine that can cut dovetails in several components simultaneously. Refer to pages 123 to 128 for more information.

CHAPTER 10

For Safety's Sake

Router users should read and observe the following instructions to ensure optimum safety conditions when they are using this power tool. The instructions are broken down into several sections: Workshop Safety; Safety Techniques for Router Components; Safety Techniques for Cutters; Safety Techniques for Routing Operations; and Safety Techniques for Freehand Operations.

WORKSHOP SAFETY

❶ Keep the workplace tidy. Remove debris and waste as part of the work program, particularly from around the feet.

❷ Arrange lighting for maximum illumination of the work area.

❸ Lock doors leading into the work area, or ask other users not to interrupt, during machining operations. Keep children out of harm's way during any operation.

❹ Use safety glasses (or, if an eyeglass-wearer, goggles, over the normal eyeglasses) to protect against flying shrapnel from particles of broken tips or shards of hard material. A transparent visor is probably even better, but it must be kept scrupulously clean (10–1 and 10–2).

❺ Earmuffs should be worn to protect the hearing from loud and high-pitched sounds created by routing operations. If these are found to be cumbersome, earplugs are an unobtrusive and economical alternative.

❻ Remember, any kind of dust is harmful, and dust extractors are rarely equipped to cope with fine dust (they remove only heavier chips and shav-

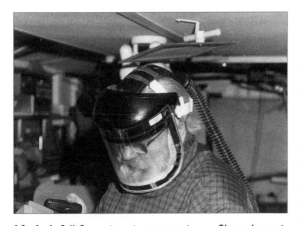

10–1. A full-face visor incorporating a filtered respirator is a desirable adjunct to conventional dust extraction.

10–2. The author wearing spectacles that are not simply bifocals, but anti-shatter lenses with surface treatment for anti-glare and ultraviolet ray protection.

(continued on following page)

WORKSHOP SAFETY (CONTINUED)

ings), so use a dust mask at all times when machining. Dust doesn't go away when the sawing stops; it is likely to remain for some time after the router has been turned off, so keep the mask on for a few minutes longer.

For any prolonged sessions, use an air filter of the kind that removes dust down to 1 micron in size.

❼ Wear strong shoes, to protect from possible damage caused by dropping sharp or heavy objects. They should have nonslip soles (10–3).

❽ Wear clothing that does not have loose or flapping pockets or sleeves. The type with hip pockets and tight cuffs worn by wood turners make good sense (10–4).

❾ Put away tools after use to avoid damaging them or causing personal injury.

❿ Store all flammable materials such as paint, varnish, polish, and cleaning supplies in a fireproof storage, such as a metal cabinet (10–5).

10–3. Strong boots with nonskid soles make sense for general wear around the workshop.

10–4. It is advisable to wear overalls for protection. This one, with a zipped front, is very practical, particularly with pockets at the rear, outside the chip-projection area.

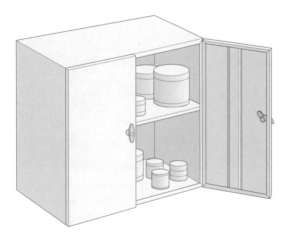

10–5. A steel cabinet for storage of any flammable materials such as paint, varnish, or polish.

SAFETY TECHNIQUES FOR ROUTER COMPONENTS

❶ Read workshop manuals and any handbook relating to the router or any machinery being used. Become familiar with all the operational controls and switch gear.

❷ Make a habit of inspecting power cables, plugs, and sockets. Any wear or damage to components in the power supply requires repair or replacement. Use plugs molded from unbreakable material. Also use cables of the correct power rating in all cases, according to the manufacturer's recommendations.

❸ See that the power cable is suspended above the work area and not likely to impede the movement of the router or be accidentally chopped up by the cutter (10–6).

❹ Beware of any insidious dampness, such as might be caused by condensation, encroaching on the electric circuitry.

❺ Make a habit of checking that all screws and nuts fitted to accessories are tightened before switching on the router (10–7).

❻ Observe the advice given in Router Care and Maintenance on pages 33 to 40; users should set up a program to suit their own machine and their use of it. Clean collets, threads, and any moving parts regularly to ensure free running and efficiency.

❼ After using a fence or other attachment for several passes, inspect all attachment screws and tighten them if necessary.

❽ See that the bench or stand is stable and that the machine, if attached to it, is attached securely by bolts or clamps.

❾ Not all machines are similar, so if an unfamiliar machine is being used, double check its features, such as switch gear, plunge lock, etc., before embarking on a routing operation.

10–6. With the power cable suspended above the workbench, hazards are reduced and movement is less restricted.

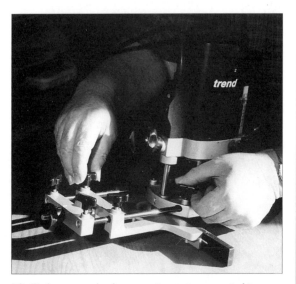

10–7. As a standard precaution prior to switching on the router, check that any nuts, screws, and bolts associated with the routing setup are secure.

SAFETY TECHNIQUES FOR CUTTERS

❶ When changing cutters, do not overtighten the collet (10–8). This can damage the cutter shank, possibly causing the cutter to become loose under stress and even dropping out of the collet, with hazardous consequences. Also, install the shank of the cutter as far into the collet as possible to ensure maximum security. Withdrawing it to give a greater depth of cut is not recommended. Keep at least two-thirds of the shank in the collet.

❷ Do not use cutters with chipped or dull cutting edges. Sharp cutters stay sharper for longer and are less likely to develop deep abrasions. Maintain edges with frequent honing.

❸ When handling cutters for any length of time as in the sharpening process, wear gloves to avoid injury to the hands. A properly honed cutting edge is sharp enough to cut flesh (refer to 10–8).

❹ Never, for any reason, bring fingers near a revolving cutter.

❺ Because excessive depth of cut causes extreme stress on collet, bearings, shaft, motor, and the cutter itself, determine, if possible, what the recommendations are for a given cutter applied to a particular material.

❻ In cases such as edge-forming, where the cutter is exposed, use a guard if one is provided or contrive one to prevent accidental contact of either the workpiece or the hands with the cutter. Often as not, the more effective the guard, the more obstructive it is to the manipulation of the router and the workpiece, but get used to it and become as good with the guard as without it!

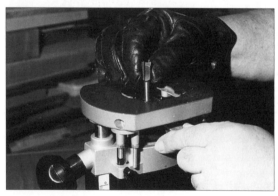

10–8. Handling cutters can be hazardous, especially during sharpening operations or when they are being fitted into collets. A pair of gloves makes sense in these situations.

SAFETY TECHNIQUES FOR ROUTING OPERATIONS

❶ Having decided on the class of work to be done, the material chosen, and the appropriate cutter selected, see that the task is within the capacity of the machine. It is bad practice to force the router beyond its reasonable limits and, moreover, it may be dangerous.

❷ Make a trial run before doing any machining.

❸ Make sure of the correct direction of feed, especially when applying the router by hand. This is not only safer, but it produces a smooth cutting action.

❹ Before starting the router, see that there is no contact between the cutter and the workpiece.

❺ Adjust hold-downs to allow secure but smooth passage of the workpiece as it traverses the cutter (10–9).

❻ Use a push stick to feed the workpiece close to the cutter.

❼ Separate the cutter from the workpiece before stopping the router.

❽ Wait until the router has stopped before attempting to move it or the workpiece. If a hand-held router is being operated, make sure that the cutter has stopped before placing the router aside to avoid its "running away" driven by the rotating cutter and causing damage.

❾ Restrict the use of the router to one pair of hands, that is, one operator at a time.

❿ After trimming soft metals or plastic laminates, a sharp burr may be left on the corners. This should be removed with a lightweight abrasive to prevent personal injury (10–10).

⓫ When constructing jigs and templates, fit metal connections into recesses to avoid contact with the hands while passing a router over them during the routing operation.

⓬ Keep workpiece thickness and cutter depth within the limits specified by the manufacturer, not only to reduce hazards but to be kind to the machine.

⓭ Before carrying out any adjustment to the machine or cutters, isolate the router from the power supply, not only by switching off at the machine but also from the main connection. Prior to reconnecting to the main power supply, see that the slide switch on the router has not been inadvertently pushed to the "on" position during cutter adjustments (10–11). This is a precaution,

SAFETY TECHNIQUES FOR ROUTING OPERATIONS (CONTINUED)

especially if the router has no NVR switch. (NVR stands for No Voltage Release, meaning that if electrical current has ceased to pass through the switch, it returns to the "off"position.)

10–10. Apart from its appearance, the workpiece is best smoothed at the corners if a sharp or burred edge is left by the cutter. Splinters can cause unpleasant personal injury, particularly from some exotic hardwoods to which the operator may be allergic.

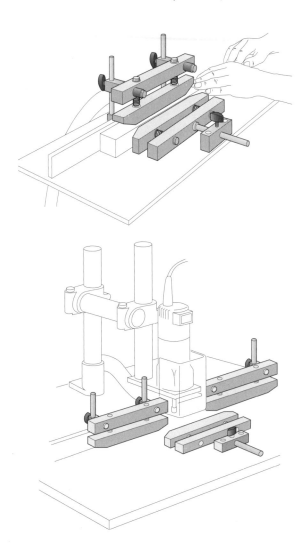

10–9. Two possible arrangements of hold-downs, one in inverted mode, the other in overhead mode. The same principles apply, to prevent lateral or upward movement of the workpiece away from the cutter. Sufficient pressure is required to hold the workpiece securely, but not so that the traversing action is impeded.

10–11. On-off switches are preferably of the NVR (No Volt Release) type. This simply means that if electrical power is discontinued, for any reason—including power failure—the switch will return to the "off" position.

SAFETY TECHNIQUES FOR FREEHAND OPERATIONS

❶ Before commencing a freehand routing operation in which the router is controlled with the hands, make sure that the power cable is clear of the machine and the path it will take during the machining process.

❷ When routing freehand, see that the feet are placed strategically to obviate the need to move them during the operation (refer to 10–6).

❸ Use clamps to provide maximum security to hold the workpiece during freehand operations, without impeding the movement of the router and arranged to permit both hands to control the router at all times (10–12).

❹ When performing freehand routing operations, be prepared to counteract the sharp snatch of the router when the motor starts up. Even with a "soft start" function—a feature on some of the newer models that allows the operator to gradually increase a router's speed—a firm grip is advised at all times.

10–12. This standard worktable is useful for clamping panels for surface routing in freehand mode.

Glossary

Acrylic Plastic material; machinable with routing cutters. Tungsten-tipped cutters are best for acrylic, which is a tough and abrasive material.

Arbor A special spindle to which may be mounted various blades for slotting or grooving. Refer to Arbor Combinations on pages 58 and 59.

Armature The rotating component in a motor.

Auxiliary Base A base made from thin material that is used to cover all or part of the original base of the router.

Back-Cutting Describes the effect when the router is fed in the same direction as the cutter is rotating. Recommended only in jig-controlled operations.

Base The part of the router that either supports or holds the motor unit. It is the contact point between the router and the work surface. Refer to Base on pages 23, 33, and 34.

Beading Cutters Cutters used for producing decorative moldings for edges of chairs, shelves, frames, and tabletops. Refer to Beading Cutters on page 51.

Bearing Guide A device fitted to a router cutter, mounted on the shank, either above or below the cutting blade.

Bench Dog A stop inserted into holes bored into bench tops that can be used to clamp many irregular shapes. Refer to Bench Dogs on pages 76 and 77.

Bit A common alternative term for a cutter. Refer to Chapter 2.

Brush A carbon tablet used to conduct electric current in contact with the commutator on a series-wound electric motor—that is, a motor in which the field and armature circuits are wound in a series. Refer to Brushes on page 39.

Burr A multi-fluted cutter used for cleaning up metals or wood. Refer to Cutters for Metals and Plastics on page 56 and to Metals on page 83.

Cam Clamp A user-made clamp that is helpful when the surface of the workpiece is being routed. Refer to Wedges and Cam Clamps on page 76.

Capillary Cutter A cutter with a radius end for making grooves in exterior woodwork, such as windows. The groove acts as a break to prevent water from flowing in.

Carbide A metal compound of carbon with an

element of calcium used in the production of the tips of some router cutters. The metal is extremely hard and somewhat brittle. Refer to Solid-Steel and Carbide-Tipped Cutters on pages 41 and 42.

Carbon Steel Steel with carbon added for hardness, often used for less expensive router cutters.

C-Clamp So-called because of its resemblance to the letter C, this is one of the most popular general-purpose clamps available. Refer to C-Clamps on page 74.

Chamfering Cutter A cutter used to relieve a corner or edge with a chamfer or a bevel. Refer to Chamfering Cutters on page 53.

Chipboard Material made from compressed wood particles. Refer to Man-Made Boards on pages 82 and 83.

Chuck A name sometimes used as an alternative to collet.

CNC (Computer Numerical Control) The name given to machinery whose operations are controlled by computer program.

Collet A circular device with at least one lateral slit to permit its closure to grip the shank of a cutter. Refer to Power and Speeds on pages 21 and 22, Collets on pages 30 to 33, and Collets (maintenance techniques for) on pages 35 and 36.

Collet Nut The nut screwed onto the end of the router spindle that retains the collet and causes it to grip or release the cutter shank.

Combination Cutter A blade holder to which may be added different tips at different positions to produce more than one shape.

Counterbore Cutter A cutter used to produce a counterbore — a second hole bored after an initial drilling of a hole that accepts a screw or bolt. This hole should be of a diameter big enough to accept the screw head. Counterbore cutters drill both the screw hole and counterbore simultaneously. Refer to Counterboring Cutters on pages 54 and 55.

Coving Cutter A cutter with a radiused bottom edge used for making channels with rounded bottoms. Refer to Coving Cutters on pages 53 and 54.

Crosscut A cut made across the grain of a wooden workpiece. Refer to Crosscutting on page 101.

Cutter Block Device for attaching replaceable or disposable cutting tips.

Cutting Diameter The maximum width of cut attainable from a single pass of any router cutter.

Cutting Length The length of a cutter's cutting edge.

Dado Trench or channel routed usually across the grain of a panel. Refer to Straight-Line Cutting on pages 99 to 101.

Depth of Cut The distance into which a cutter penetrates a workpiece.

Depth Stop On plunge routers, this device allows the depth of cut to be preset.

Double-Flute Cutter A cutter with two cutting edges and which leaves a cleaner cut surface than a single-flute cutter. This cutter is useful for many types of work, including plunge-routing and "bottoming" grooves. Refer to Double-Flute Cutters on page 47.

Dovetail Joint An extremely strong joint used to join the sides and ends of boxes, drawers, and many kinds of cabinets. Refer to Dovetail Joint on pages 103 and 104.

False Fence A jig made of wood that is attached to the fence of the router or router table. The wooden face allows precise shaping to fit the router cutter profile and thus better support the work.

Feed Rate The speed at which the routing operation is being performed, either by the router cutter moving into the workpiece or vice versa. Refer to Chapter 6.

Fence A guide, adjustable to suit different widths, attached to a router or to a router table. It ensures parallel control of the edge of a workpiece and the cutter's path.

Fiberglass (also referred to as glass fiber) A board comprised of fibrous material that can be cut with metal cutters. Refer to Plastics and Related Laminates on page 84.

Fine Adjuster An auxiliary tool for the fine adjustment of the depth stop on a plunge router.

Fixed-Base Router A router whose distance between the base and motor unit cannot be altered during routing operations. Plunge routers can be locked in a fixed position to produce the same effect. Refer to Fixed-Base Routers on pages 18 and 19.

Fixed Routing When a router is mounted in a device to hold it securely in either an overhead or inverted position. In this case, the workpiece is taken to the router. Refer to Fixed-Router Techniques on pages 87 to 91.

Flute The gap between cutting edges through which waste material escapes. Refer to Chapter 2.

Frame Jig A frame for guiding a router either inside or outside its periphery, usually made to special dimensions.

Gasket A pressure-sensitive air seal.

Grooving Cutter A V-shaped cutter used to cut grooves and chamfers of various widths and to engrave. Refer to Grooving Cutters on page 55.

Ground The floor or foundation of a carving exposed by routing around a motif to a uniform depth.

GRP (Glass-reinforced polyester, or fiberglass) A glass in fibrous form that is used in woodworking applications and can be cut with a router. Refer to Plastics and Related Laminates on page 84.

Guard A safety device used to prevent the fingers of the router operator from making contact with the cutter. Refer to Safety Techniques for Cutters on page 142.

Guide Bearing A device fitted to a router cutter, mounted on the shank either above or below the cutting blade.

Guide Bush A hollow ring formed in the center of a plate that is attached to the base of a router. The cutter is inserted through the ring that then becomes a bearing used to follow a template while the workpiece is machined by the cutter. Refer to Guide Bushes on pages 111 to 113.

Hardboard A material generally used for drawer bottoms, panel backing, and siding and cabinet parts. Refer to Man-Made Boards on pages 82 and 83.

Hold-Down An important device used to hold

the workpiece down against the surface of a router table while machining is in progress. Refer to Hold-Downs on pages 76 and 77 and Safety Techniques for Routing Operations on pages 142 and 143.

Hone To sharpen cutting edges with oilstones for solid-steel cutters and diamond stones for cutters with tungsten-carbide tips. Refer to Sharpening Cutters on pages 62 to 64.

Horizontal Routing A variation on inverted routing, in which the router is used lying on its side, its spindle horizontal and the base of the router at right angles to the router table. The advantages of this technique for certain operations are excellent visibility of the routing action, good waste clearance, and more increased control of the workpiece. Refer to Horizontal Routing on page 94.

Horsepower (hp) A term used to describe the amount of physical energy used by a router. Refer to Power on pages 21 and 22.

HSS (High Speed Steel) Steel made from a high-carbon-content steel used frequently for router cutters.

Inlaying The technique of setting in hinges and other hardware. This requires the cutting of shallow recesses into a surface, which can be done with inlaying cutters. Refer to Inlaying Cutters on page 57 and Inlaying on page 108.

Inverted Routing A technique in which the base of the router is uppermost and, consequently, is attached to some device to maintain that position during a routing operation. Refer to Inverting Routing on pages 87 to 91.

Jig A common name for a device, often user-made, to hold a router or a workpiece. It also serves a purpose if repetition work is required. Refer to Chapter 9.

Kerf The slot or gap made by the cutter.

MDF (Medium-Density Fiberboard) A common man-made panel made from wood-based material. LDF (Low-Density Fiberboard) is also available. Refer to Man-Made Boards on pages 82 and 83.

Molding A strip of material generally of decorative section used to cover or trim some joint or partition. Refer to Molding Cutters on page 50 and Edge Treatments on page 106.

Mortise A square or rectangular recess machined in a workpiece to match a tenon on a separate member to enable the joining of the two pieces. Refer to Mortise Cutters on page 57 and Mortise-and-Tenon Joint on pages 101 to 103.

NVR Switch (No Voltage Release) A safety feature on a router that switches "off" if the main electrical power is disconnected. Refer to Chapter 10.

Overhead Routing When a router is fixed to a bracket in its normal position with the cutter pointing down, it is said to be in "overhead" mode, and overhead routing can then be performed. This means that the workpiece may be passed beneath the router to perform the routing operation. Refer to Overhead Routing on pages 91 to 93.

Ovolo Cutters Used for the production of rounded convex moldings and the rounding-over of panels and edge molding. Refer to Ovolo Cutters on page 58.

Panel-Raising Cutter Used to reduce the edge of a panel to the thickness required for insertion into the grooved frame of a cabinet door. Refer to Panel-Raising Cutters on page 51.

Particleboard Sheet material made from wood chips.

Pass Taken to mean one transit of a cutter across a workpiece.

Pin Routing An overhead routing technique in which a captive pin inserted into the router table in line with and beneath the router spindle acts as a guide against which the workpiece is moved with its upper edge in contact with the cutter. Refer to Pin Routing on pages 93 and 94.

Plug Cutter A special-purpose cutter used to produce a plug of the correct diameter to match a counterbored hole. Refer to Plug Cutters on page 54.

Plunge Descriptive reference given to the action of a router whose motor slides on spring-loaded columns to achieve the so-called "plunge" action.

Plywood Plies of wood glued together in a sandwich-like fashion that are used for general and furniture construction. Refer to Man-Made Boards on pages 82 and 83.

Profile An outline of a section or contour.

Profile Scriber A special set of cutters used in conjunction to produce matching members for frame construction. Refer to Profile Scribers on page 50.

PVA (Polyvinyl Acetate Adhesive) Commonly known as "white" glue, this adhesive is suitable for most woodworking joints.

Quick-Action Clamp General-purpose clamp that occupies less space, has greater maneuverability, and is faster to apply than a C-clamp. Refer to Quick-Action Clamps on pages 74 and 75.

Rabbet (Rebate) An open-sided groove running along an edge. Refer to Rabbet Cutters on page 53.

Radial Relief The amount of clearance behind the cutting edge of a cutter that prevents friction between the bit and the cut surface. Refer to Radial Relief on pages 42 and 43.

Rake (Hook) Angle The angle made by the tip face on a cutter to the centerline of the cutter body. Refer to Rake Angle on pages 42 and 43.

Rate of Feed See Feed Rate.

Recessing Cutter A cutter designed for cutting recesses in the end and face of a workpiece in a plunge mode. Refer to Recessing Cutters on page 56.

Reversible-Tip Cutter A cutter whose tip is attached to the cutter body by screws and is both reversible, allowing the use of a second edge when the first has become dulled, and replaceable when both edges are blunt. Refer to Reversible-Tip Cutters on page 58.

Ring Fence A safety device used for a fixed inverted router in spindle-molding operations.

Rip Cut A cut made in line with or along the grain.

Rosette (Roundel) Shapers Cutters used to produce floral designs in wood used as decorative elements. Refer to Rosette Shapers on page 58.

Rotary Turret The rotary turret has a circular base fixed by a spring-loaded pin in its center to allow it to rotate. Rotation of the turret brings one of the "stops," usually three, to vertical alignment with the depth-stop rod. Refer also to Turret Stop in this section and Rotary Turrets on pages 28 to 30.

Router Table A table to which a router is attached, either underneath or above the work surface and upon which the work is supported during machining operations. Router tables can be commercial or user-made. Refer to Inverted Routing on pages 87 to 91.

Self-Guiding Cutter A cutter with a bearing mounted on its shank, either above or below the cutting blade. The intention is that the bearing follows the edge of a template while the blade cuts the required workpiece to shape. Refer to Self-Guiding Cutters on pages 48 and 49.

Shank A cutter's plain cylindrical stem of an exact diameter to fit the appropriate collet, by which it is gripped. Refer to Shank on page 44.

Shear Cutter A cutter whose cutting edge is said to be "positive," or angled downwards. This produces the effect known as "down-cutting," a function that produces a clean cut edge. Refer to Shear Angle on pages 42 and 43 and Direction of Feed on pages 96 and 97.

Side Clearance The difference between a cutter's tip diameter and body. Refer to Side Clearance on page 44.

Side Fence A guide attached to a router by means of a pair of rods that slide into the router base and used for parallel grooving or cutting. Refer to Freehand Routing on pages 85 to 87.

Single-Flute Cutter Cutter with a single cutting edge which is good for roughing out blank workpieces in preparation for template work and plunge-cutting, boring holes, etc. Refer to Single-Flute Cutters on pages 46 and 47.

Ski Bars A pair of bars arranged on either side of the router, resulting in extending the normal width of the router base. Refer to Chapter 9.

Slot Cutter A cutter frequently fitted on arbors for multiple grooving applications. Refer to Slot Cutters on page 58.

Socket Clamp A clamp with a round projecting plug instead of a pressure pad, which is inserted into the edge of a workpiece and clamped. Useful for securing workpieces without protruding above the surface. Refer to Socket Clamps on page 76.

Spindle Lock A device fitted to the router spindle to temporarily prevent its rotation while tightening or loosening the collet nut. Refer to Collets on pages 35 and 36.

Spiral Cutters Straight cutters with spiral designs intended for a wide variety of applications but especially for cutting and trimming panels. Spiral-flute cutters can be used for laminates and plastics and for most solid-wood projects. Refer to Spiral-Flute Cutters on pages 47 and 48.

Staggered-Tooth Cutter A cutter with several tips arranged at different positions to permit clearance of waste when boring deep recesses.

Stop An appliance to prevent further travel of a workpiece that is being slid into position, or a similar device that allows movement of a router until contact is made with the stop and its movement is terminated. The name is also given to the termination of any movement of a component part or the device that prevents its movement.

Straight Cutter Has straight cutting edges and parallel flutes and can be used for many applications, including cutting grooves, dadoes, slots, mortises, recesses, and removing waste. Refer to Straight Cutters on pages 46 to 48.

Sub-Base An auxiliary base attached temporarily to the base of the router, either to increase the base area or to attach the machine to a table.

TCT (Tungsten-Carbide Tipped) Refers to the tips of cutters made of tungsten carbide, which is harder than HSS or carbon steel. The tips are brazed onto the base steel cutter.

Template A pattern shaped to function as a guide in conjunction with a bearing-guided cutter or a guide bush. Attached temporarily to a workpiece, the edge of the template is then followed by the bearing or bush as the cutter machines the workpiece. Refer to Chapter 7.

Tenon A projection, about one-third the thickness of a member, designed to fit into a matching recess, called a mortise, for the purpose of joining the two parts. Refer to Cutting a Tenon on pages 102 and 103.

Toggle Clamp A clamp available in a wide variety of designs employing the principles of mechanical movement that involves pivots, levers, and over-center clamping actions. It can be rapidly used in repetitive routing applications.

Refer to Toggle Clamps on page 75.

Trimming Cutter A cutter designed specially for trimming, such as overhanging laminate or veneer from panels. Refer to Trimming Cutters on pages 52 and 53.

Tungsten A metal found chiefly in the mineral wolframite and combined with carbide to increase its durability. It is the material from which the tips of some cutters are made.

Turret Stop One of three so-called "stops" making up a feature of the depth-control system on a router. Quick-change depth stops can be preset with this facility. Refer also to Rotary Turret in this section.

Vacuum Clamping A system of clamping operated by creating a vacuum between the workpiece and a flat surface with sealed cells. The cells have a rubber-based edging and an orifice connected by tube to an extractor, similar to a vacuum cleaner. A practical answer to the problem of holding a workpiece without the impedance of conventional clamping. Refer to Vacuum Clamping on pages 78 to 80.

Wedge A user-made clamp designed for surface routing. Refer to Wedges and Cam Clamps on page 76.

Metric Equivalents Chart

INCHES TO MILLIMETERS AND CENTIMETERS

MM— Millimeters   CM—Centimeters

Inches	MM	CM	Inches	CM	Inches	CM
1/8	3	0.3	9	22.9	30	76.2
1/4	6	0.6	10	25.4	31	78.7
3/8	10	1.0	11	27.9	32	81.3
1/2	13	1.3	12	30.5	33	83.8
5/8	16	1.6	13	33.0	34	86.4
3/4	19	1.9	14	35.6	35	88.9
7/8	22	2.2	15	38.1	36	91.4
1	25	2.5	16	40.6	37	94.0
1¼	32	3.2	17	43.2	38	96.5
1½	38	3.8	18	45.7	39	99.1
1¾	44	4.4	19	48.3	48	101.6
2	51	5.1	20	50.8	41	104.1
2½	64	6.4	21	53.3	42	106.7
3	76	7.6	22	55.9	43	109.2
3½	89	8.9	23	58.4	44	111.8
4	102	10.2	24	61.0	45	114.3
4½	114	11.4	25	63.5	46	116.8
5	127	12.7	25	66.0	47	119.4
6	152	15.2	27	68.6	48	121.9
7	178	17.8	28	71.1	49	124.5
8	203	20.3	29	73.7	50	127.0

Currently Available Routers

Make and Model	Power	Speed (rpm)		Collet Sizes				Adjustable Depth	Weight (approx.)
FIXED-BASED ROUTERS									
	hp	single	variable	¼ inch	⅜ inch	8 mm	½ inch	(inches)	(lbs)
Bosch 1617	1.75	25,000		yes	yes	yes	yes	1.875	7.5
Bosch 1618	1.75	25,000		yes	yes	yes	yes	1.875	8
Bosch 1617 EVS	2		8-25,000	yes	yes	yes	yes	1.875	7.7
Craftsman 17504	1.5	25,000		yes				1.5	7.5
Craftsman 17505	1.75		15-25,000	yes				1.5	8.3
Craftsman 27500	2	25,000		yes			yes	1.5	9.1
DeWalt DW610	1.5	25,000		yes			yes	2.375	7.3
Makita 3606	1	30,000		yes				3	5.5
Milwaukee 5660	1.5	24,500		yes	yes		yes	2.25	8.5
Milwaukee 5680	2	26,000		yes	yes		yes	2.25	8.8
Milwaukee 5681	2	26,000		yes	yes		yes	2.25	8.8
Milwaukee 5682	2	26,000		yes	yes		yes	2.25	8.8
Porter-Cable 100	.875	22,000		yes				1.5	6.8
Porter-Cable 690	1.5	23,000		yes	yes		yes	1.5	8
Porter-Cable 691	1.5	23,000		yes	yes		yes	1.5	9.3
Porter-Cable 7536	2.5	21,000		yes	yes		yes	2.5	14.5
Porter-Cable 7537	2.5	21,000		yes	yes		yes	2.5	14.5
Porter-Cable 7518	3.5		10-21,000	yes	yes		yes	2.5	14.5
Porter-Cable 7519	3.25	21,000		yes	yes		yes	2.5	15
Ryobi R160	1.5	25,000		yes				1.5	7.5
Ryobi 7165k	1.75	25,000		yes				1.5	8
Ryobi RE170	1.75		15-25,000	yes			yes	1.5	8.8
Ryobi R180	2	25,000		yes			yes	1.5	8.8
Ryobi RE185	2.25		15-20,000	yes			yes	2.5	9

PLUNGE ROUTERS

Make and Model	Power		Speed (rpm)		inches			mm			Plunge Depth	Weight (approx.)
	hp*	watt**	single	variable	¼	⅜	½	6	8	12	inches	lbs.
AEG OFE630		630		10-27,500	yes***						2	7.25
AEG OFS720		720	25,000		yes		opt****	opt			2	5.5
AEG OFSE850		850		8-25,000			yes	opt	opt		2	5.5
AEG OFSE2000		720		8-24,000	opt		yes		opt		3	5.5
Atlas Copco OFSE720		720	25,000		yes			yes	yes		2	5.5
Atlas Copco OFSE850		850		8-24,000	yes			yes	yes		2	6
Atlas Copco OFSE 2000		2,000		8-24,000			yes		yes	yes	3	11.5
Black & Decker KW 780		600	30,000		yes			yes	yes	yes	2.25	6.5
Black & Decker KW 780E		600		8-30,000	yes			yes	yes		2.25	6.5
Bosch POF 400A		400	27,000		yes			opt	opt		2	4
Bosch POF 500A		500	27,000		yes			opt	opt		2	4.75
Bosch POF 600ACE		600		12-27,000	yes			opt	opt		2	4.5
Bosch GOF 900ACE		900		12-24,000	yes			opt	opt		2	7.75
Bosch GOF 1300ACE		1300	12,000		yes	opt	yes	opt	opt	opt	2.375	9.6
Bosch GOF 1600A		1600	25,000		yes	opt	yes	opt	opt	opt	3	12.5
Bosch 1613EVS	2			12-22,000	yes	yes	yes		yes		2	10
Bosch 1614EVS	1.25			12-23,000	yes						2	8
Bosch 1615	3		25,000		yes	yes	yes				3	12
Bosch 1615EVS	3.25			12-23,000	yes	yes	yes				3	12.3
Bosch GOF 1700ACE		1700		8-23,000	yes	opt	yes	opt	opt	opt	3	12.75
Craftsman 17507	1.75			15-25,000	yes						2	8.4
Craftsman 27510	2		22,000		yes		yes				2.5	11.5
Craftsman 2751i	3.5			10-22,000	yes		yes				2.5	13
DeWalt DW613		800	27,000		yes			opt	opt		1.375	6
DeWalt DW620		750	24,000		yes			opt	opt		2.25	6
DeWalt DW620L		900	24,000		yes			opt	opt		2.25	6.75
DeWalt DW621		1100		8-24,000	yes			opt	opt		2.25	7.25
DeWalt DW625		1850	20,000		yes		yes	opt	opt	opt	2.25	11.25
DeWalt DW625L		1850		8-20,000	yes	opt	yes	opt	opt	opt	2.625	11.25
DeWalt DW621KL		1100		8-24,000	yes			opt	opt		2.25	7

(continued on following page)

PLUGE ROUTERS (CONTINUED)											
Make and Model	Power		Speed (rpm)		inches			mm			Plunge Depth	Weight
	hp*	watt**	single	variable	¼	⅜	½	6	8	12	inches	lbs.
Einhell EOF 850SP		850	24,000		yes				yes		2	NA
Elu MOF 96		750	24,000		yes			opt	opt		2.25	6
Elu MOF 96E		900		8-24,000	yes			opt	opt		2.25	6.5
Elu OF 97		900	24,000		yes			opt	opt		2.25	7.25
Elu OF 97EK		1100		8-24,000	yes			opt	opt		2.25	7.25
Elu MOF 131		1300	22,000		yes			opt	opt	opt	2.5	9.5
Elu MOF 177		1600	20,000		yes		yes	opt	opt	opt	2.5	11.25
Elu MOF 177EK		1850	20,000		yes		yes	opt	opt	opt	2.5	11.25
Festo OF 900 Plus		900	26,500		yes			opt	yes		2	6
Festo OF 900E Plus		900		10-22,000	yes			opt	yes		2	6
Festo FO 1000E Plus	1.5			10-20,000	yes				yes		1.75	6
Festo OF2000 Plus		1800	25,000		opt	opt	opt	opt	yes	yes	2.5	11.25
Freud FT2000E		1900		8-22,000	yes	opt	yes				2.75	13.25
Hitachi ZK 2008		550	27,000		yes						2	4.75
Hitachi M8		800	25,000		yes						2	6
Hitachi M8V		800		10-25,000	yes						2	6
Hitachi M12SA		1600	22,000		yes	opt	yes				2.375	11.5
Hitachi M12V		1850		8-20,000	yes	opt	yes				2.375	11.5
Hitachi TR12	3		22,000		yes	yes	yes				2.437	11.3
Holzher 2355		800	25,000		yes						2	6
Holzher 2356		1010		8-25,000	yes						2	6
Mafell LO 50E		900		10-22,000	yes	opt		opt	yes		2	6
Mafell LO 65E		1800		8-20,000	opt			opt	yes	opt	2.5	12
Makita 3620		860	24,000		yes	yes					1.375	4.75
Makita 3612BR		1600	23,000		yes	yes	yes				2.375	12.5
Makita 3612C		1850		9-23,000	yes	yes	yes	opt	opt	opt	2.375	11
Makita 3612		1850	22,000		yes	yes	yes				2.375	12.75
Metabo OF1028		1010	27,000		yes			opt	opt		2	7.25
Metabo OFE 1229 Signal		1200	27,000		yes			opt	opt		2	7.5
Metabo OF1612		1600	24,000		opt	opt	yes	opt	opt		3.25	11

(continued on following page)

Make and Model	Power		Speed (rpm)		inches			mm			Plunge Depth	Weight
	hp*	watt**	single	variable	¼	⅜	½	6	8	12	inches	lbs.
Metabo OF528		500	27,000		yes			opt	opt		2	6.5
Perles OF 808		850	25,000						yes		2	6
Porter-Cable OFT3 12VV		1680		10-21,000			yes				2.875	17.25
Porter-Cable 7538	3.25		21,000		yes	yes	yes				3	17.3
Porter-Cable 7539	3.25			10-21,000	yes	yes	yes				3	17.3
Porter-Cable 693	1.5		23,000		yes	yes	yes				2.5	11.5
Ryobi RE120		570		17-28,000	yes						2.25	4.75
Ryobi R151		750	27,000		yes			yes	opt		2	6
Ryobi RE155K		800		10-27,000	yes				opt		2	6.5
Ryobi R175	1.75		25,000		yes						2	8.1
Ryobi RE175	1.75			15-25,000	yes						2	8.1
Ryobi R502		1600	25,000		yes	yes	yes	yes	yes		2.375	11
Ryobi R600N		2050	23,000		yes	yes	yes	yes	yes		2.375	13.5
Ryobi RE600N		2050		10-23,000	yes	yes	yes	yes	yes		2.375	13.5
Skil 1823	1.5		25,000		yes						2	7
Skil 1840	1.75		25,000		yes						2	7
Skil 1845-02	2			8-25,000	yes						2	7.3
Skil 1845-44	2			8-25,000	yes						2	7.3
Skil 1875U1		1400		8-22,000	yes		yes				2.375	5.10
Trend T5		850		9-27,000	yes	opt	yes	opt	opt	opt	2	6
Trend T9		1800		8-22,000	yes	no	no	no	yes		3	11.5
Virutex FR77C		850	24,000			opt		opt	yes		2	6.75
Virutex FR78C		850		8-24,000	opt			opt	yes		2	6.75
Woodcut TC-1800E		1800		8-24,000	opt	opt	yes	opt	opt		3.5	11.25

* Routers designated by horsepower are those currently available in the United States.

** Routers designated by watts are European models.

*** Included in router package.

**** Is available as an optional extra.

Index